A STUDENT'S
GUIDE TO THE
INTERNET

A STUDENT'S GUIDE TO THE INTERNET

Surfing for Success in Management

1998 - 1999

Contributors:
Marian B. Wood
Raymond D. Frost,
Central Connecticut State University
Judy Strauss,
Central Connecticut State University
Andrew T. Stull

Prentice Hall
Upper Saddle River, NJ 07458

Development: *Joan Waxman, Audrey Regan, and Steve Deitmer*
Interior design and formatting: *Theresa Festa*
Cover design: *Lorraine Castellano*
Advertising copy and design: *Eve Adams*
Production manager: *Richard Bretan*

© 1999 by Prentice Hall, Inc.
A Simon & Schuster Company
Upper Saddle River, New Jersey 07458

Printed in the United States of America

10 9 8 7 6 5 4 3 2

ISBN 0-13-081525-X

TRADEMARK INFORMATION
Netscape and Netscape Navigator are registered trademarks of Netscape Communications Corporation in the United States and other countries. Netscape's logos and Netscape product and service names are also trademarks of Netscape Communications Corporation, which may be registered in other countries. Other product and brand names are trademarks of their respective owners.

DIGITAL, AltaVista, and the AltaVista logo are trademarks or service marks of Digital Equipment Corporation. Used in permission.

Text and artwork copyright © 1998 by Yahoo! Inc. All rights reserved. Yahoo! and the Yahoo! logo are trademarks of Yahoo! Inc.

Screen shots reprinted with permission from the following companies and organizations:
Resumix®, Inc., a subsidiary of Ceridian Corporation
Metacrawler^{SM}, go2net, Inc.
University of Phoenix, CPE*Internet*
The Marketing Resource Center, Concept Marketing Group Inc.
Academy of Management Online
WorkNet@ILR, School of Industrial and Labor Relations, Cornell University

What's Inside

Preface

Chapter 1 | **Frequently Asked Questions**
What is the Internet?
How did the Net develop?
Just how popular is the Net today?
Where is the Internet?
How is the Internet organized?
Who is out there?
How do I connect to the Internet?
And what sort of ISP should a business consider?
Why are there mistakes in this book?
How do I know that an online source is credible?
How does plagiarism apply to information from online sources?
So where do I go for more information?

Chapter 2 | **Up and Running: The Search is On**
Cruising the Net
Return Visit
Go and History
Asking for Directions
Search Strategies
Why so many search engines?
Subject Tree Index
Open Text Search
Advanced Search
Pluses and Minuses
Keep it Together; Keep it in Quotes
WHEN IN DOUBT, lowercase
A Star for the Wildcard
Who is linked to us?

Chapter 3 | **Getting Your Message Out in Style: E-Mail and Other Enhancements**
Staying in Touch with E-Mail
Newsgroups
Chat
Mailing Lists
Language for the Road
There's Always Room to Improve

JavaScript and Java
Customizing

Chapter 4   **Online Job Searches and Résumés**

How to Research Careers and Employers
How to Find Job Openings
How to Create an Electronic Résumé
How to Contact Employers Online

Chapter 5   **Distance Learning**

What is distance learning?
Advantages and Disadvantages
How to Find Information About Distance Learning
A Distance Learning Sampler
10 Questions to Ask Before You Register
Learning Cyberspace

Chapter 6   **Using the Internet in your Management Course**

Sources of Management Information
Management Topics
Managing Your Management Career
The Internet as a Management Learning Tool

Appendix I   **Business-Related Internet Addresses**

Appendix II   **Glossary**

Preface

The Internet is growing fast. We are in the middle of a story with an unpredictable outcome. Businesses and individuals are jumping on the electronic-communications bandwagon at an incredible rate. Still, some critics call the Net a fad. It's been some time since we've had something this exciting to debate!

We believe that the Internet will prove to be an extremely useful tool for your education and for business planning and operations across the globe. The Internet search capabilities and resource sites can aid any discipline by opening a high-speed gateway to a wealth of information. Also, the Net can assist with text-based communication: one-to-one e-mail conversation and e-mail conferencing via newsgroups and mailing lists, for example. Whether you're giving or receiving, the Internet can serve you well. And the more you know about how it works, the more the Internet can help you. We hope this guide answers your questions and gets you as excited about the Internet as we are.

We've set up our Internet guide this way:

Chapter 1   Frequently Asked Questions (FAQs)
Through its question-and-answer format, this chapter introduces you to the Internet and gives you a taste of where it comes from and what makes it tick.

Chapter 2   Up and Running: The Search is On
From basic searches to more advanced investigations, this chapter teaches you how to reach out across the Internet to find what you need.

Chapter 3   Getting Your Message Out in Style: E-Mail and Other Enhancements
Turn here to learn how to operate e-mail through your Internet connection. And do you need to know more about chat rooms, newsgroups, mailing lists? Do you want to customize your browser? This chapter will help you out.

Chapter 4   Online Job Searches and Résumés
Filled with Internet addresses, this chapter tells you how to create an electronic résumé and get started on finding that perfect job.

Chapter 5   Distance Learning
What do you look for in an online class? We take a look at distance learning in general, then follow a student taking a class over the Internet.

Chapter 6   Using the Internet in Your Management Course
Look over this in-depth presentation of how the Internet can help you as you move through your course of study in Management.

Appendix 1 Business-Related Internet Addresses
This appendix organizes a wealth of Internet addresses by business discipline.

Appendix 2 Glossary
We give you what you need to speak the Internet language.

Chapter 1
Frequently Asked Questions (FAQs)

Many sites on the Internet use the Frequently Asked Questions (FAQ) format to help guide users and give them quick, useful answers to common questions. Often the FAQ page opens with a list of those questions that the people who built the page believe will be on many users minds. Very often, these questions contain a hot button — a hyperlink — to the answer. Users scan the list for a question they would like answered and then jump to the answer. We have kept our printed FAQ list especially small so that you can jump in and get started. Once you develop search skills from the early exercises in this book, you won't need us to answer your questions: You'll be able to search the Net yourself.

What is the Internet?

The Internet—often called simply "the Net"—is a network of computers reaching every country in the world. It is similar in some ways to the telephone system. Just as you can call people anywhere in the world, so too can you contact their computers as long as they are connected to the Net. But the Internet is more than computers and their contents: It is a social space where users communicate. It is this feature, as well as the fact that there is no governing body, that allows users to shape the Net. The Net is truly a grassroots development.

How did the Net develop?

The Internet has been around since the 1960s, when the Defense Department set it up as a fail-safe way of relaying messages in case of a nuclear attack. As a result the Internet is quite robust—communications almost always go through – though at times rather slowly. From the '60s until the early '90s the Internet's main users were the Defense Department and researchers in industry and education. These people plugged into the Net to share access to distant supercomputers and to send electronic mail. In those days, the Net was fairly hard to use and it was difficult to find your way around. Outside of a fairly small community, not that many people knew of, or cared much about, the Internet. All that changed in the mid-'90s.

Three major developments have revolutionized the way we use the Internet: the birth of the World Wide Web (WWW or Web), hyperlinks, and graphical browsers. Even though we use the terms "Internet" and "Web" interchangeably, the Web is a part of the Internet. It began as a standard that defined how to travel from computer to computer throughout the world by following embedded links in a screen display of written words (text). A click on the link and you were instantly transported to another computer as directed by the embedded instruction. Such clickable text was called hypertext. The Web and hypertext made it easy to get around because they formed a basis for navigation in cyberspace. What was missing however were pictures, icons, and color. People like a graphical interface because it is intuitive and easy to master. The development of graphical browsers solved this problem. Browsers are software programs that view information on the Internet. The most prominent browsers are Netscape Navigator (or Communicator) and Microsoft Internet Explorer. Graphical browsers allow users to click on images as well as text links to navigate in a multimedia world. Not only can sites contain text and graphics, but they can also contain sound, video and even 3D video. Graphical browsers have brought visual appeal and entertainment value to the Web. The Web, hyperlinks, and graphical browsers have made cyberspace a very friendly place and have driven the rush to get connected.

Just how popular is the Net today?

People are connecting to the Net at a phenomenal rate, and the number of Web sites is doubling every 50 days. But this rush to the Net has created two problems.

First, the Internet is becoming slow. If 10 people use the same line, they each get one-tenth of the line's capacity (or bandwidth). If 100 people use the same line, then their share is cut to one-hundredth. Similarly, the computers with Web sites on the Internet – computers we call content providers – can be overworked by the increase in users. A computer that can handle 10 people simultaneously accessing its content may come to its knees when 100 people try accessing it at the same time. Popularity in cyberspace comes with a price!

Second, the Net contains so much material that it has become difficult for users to find their way around. Fortunately, there are tools that help. These are known as search engines, and they find Net destinations for you. Knowing how to use search engines well is an essential survival skill in cyberspace. Consequently, we'll take a look at this topic soon.

Where is the Internet?

The Internet is everywhere.

Because a person can get on the Internet through a standard phone line, the Internet is anywhere in the world that one can find a telephone. Once a user connects to an Internet computer, that computer serves as a gateway to the rest of the global network. Computers offering services on the Internet are scattered throughout the world. Fortunately, users do not need to know their geographic whereabouts while on the Net. All the user needs is the Internet address, also known as the URL (Universal Resource Locator), of the computer. For example, the Internet address of the Central Connecticut State University (CCSU) School of Business (SB) is:

wwwsb.ccsu.edu

Reading backward from the end of the address, we discover that it is an educational institution (edu) within the Central Connecticut State University campus (CCSU), and that it is the World Wide Web (WWW) server of the School of Business (SB).

Most Internet addresses are not nearly so revealing as to location. It is not that the service is trying to conceal its location, but rather that location does not really matter. For example, does it matter to the user making an airline reservation that

www.americanair.com

is located in Oklahoma? Similarly, the user doesn't usually know the location of a business when dialing an 800 number. Internet addresses are like 800 numbers. One major difference: 800 numbers are normally valid only in North America, but Internet addresses are valid anywhere in the world.

How is the Internet organized?

Net addresses carry one of several major Internet address classifications, known as top-level domain names. These appear as the last item in an address – for example, the ".edu" that appears in the school address and the ".com" in the airline address we just presented. These domain names tell you the type of site you are connecting to. The following are important top-level domain names:

```
.com    commercial
.edu    educational
.gov    government
.net    Internet service provider
.org    non-profit organization
```

Knowing the domain names may help you as you search the Net. You can often guess a site address by using the organization name and domain name. For example, the site for Coca-Cola is www.coca-cola.com.
You also will see Web sites which end with letters such as ".jp", ".fr", or ".uk". These domain names indicate the country in which the Web site is located. Thus, ".jp" represents Japan, ".fr" represents France, and ".uk" represents the United Kingdom. Moreover, several additional top-level domain names have recently been approved. Don't be surprised if you see Web sites with top-level domain names like ".sport" and ".games" in the near future.

Who is out there?

We have compared the Internet to the telephone system: a global communication network of computers. But who is sitting there, hunched over a keyboard, using these computers? Content providers, advertisers, and the audience.

Content Providers
First are the content providers. These are the businesses, universities, governments, and other organizations that allow others to peek into their computers. For example, Central Connecticut State University houses a Windows NT computer, called a Web server, in the School of Business. This computer runs 24 hours a day and contains files that the school created for others to view. For example, there is information about the school's faculty and programs.

Advertisers
Second are advertisers. These are the corporations that pay content providers for space on their Web pages. For example, when you log on to a search engine's home page (search engines are the "telephone books" of the Internet), you generally will see announcements from advertisers who are paying for the space. This is how the search engines are able to offer their services for free. Toping the list is the Yahoo! search site with annual sales approaching $70 million. But even a small game site like Happy Puppy can earn $1.5 million a year selling ads. The top 50 advertisers spend over $180 million a year on ads. Leading the list is Microsoft, with expenditures of $30 million.

Audience
Finally, there is the audience. These are the people who travel the Web to find information from content providers that will be useful or entertaining. In addition to pulling data from Web servers, the audience also uses the Internet to communicate to other people via e-mail, to post messages to newsgroups, and to just sit back and surf the Net for personal pleasure.

How do I connect to the Internet?

Users surf the Net from home, business, school, or the library, almost always for a fee. In businesses, schools, and libraries the organization often pays the charge and even provides the computers. Home users must provide their own computers and pay their own way. Every Internet connection goes through an Internet Service Provider (ISP). See Figure 1.1. These organizations buy very high bandwidth connections to the Internet backbone and then resell it (many times over) in smaller pieces to subscribers. America Online, Prodigy, and Earthlink and are examples of ISPs.

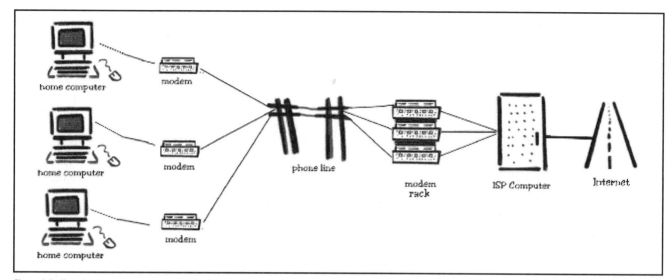

Figure 1.1 Your home computer connects to the Internet through an Internet Service Provider (ISP).

The connection from home to the ISP is typically over a phone line using a device called a modem. The modem translates the computer signals to sound waves, which are then decoded by a modem connected to a computer at the ISP receiving the call. Modems are an inexpensive means of getting connected, but they are slow. Recent technological advances allow modems to receive information off the Internet at a rate of over 50,000 characters per second. And while 50,000 characters per second is faster than any of us can read, consider what it take to handle graphics. A full-screen picture can easily exceed 1,000,000 characters (bytes), and full-motion video requires changing that picture approximately 30 times per second. Fortunately, some clever techniques (called algorithms) compress graphics, sound, and video so that they can travel over the phone lines.

Recently, some cable companies have begun to offer high speed Internet service over cable TV wire using a device called a cable modem. The cable TV wire into your home has a much greater bandwidth than a telephone line and allows for high quality video. The market will determine whether this becomes a viable option.

The home user needs communication software and a Web browser. The software controls the modem and maintains a connection with the ISP. Web browsers such as Netscape's Navigator and Microsoft's Internet Explorer offer a graphical user interface to access information on the Internet over the established network connection.

The communication channel that organizations use typically offers a faster connection to the Internet and requires different hardware and software. Organizations typically have a higher speed line (greater bandwidth) into the Internet (see Figure 1.2). However, since the high speed line is shared, as the number of users in the organization increases, the speed with which each communicates decreases accordingly.

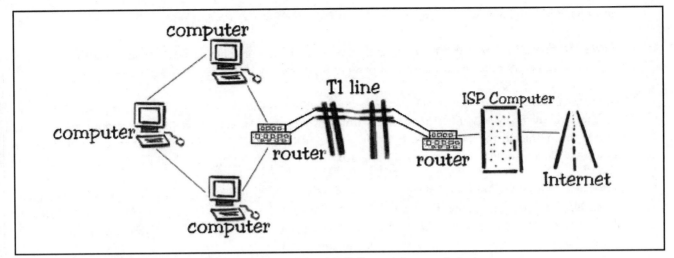

Figure 1.2 In many businesses, signals from individual computers travel through a T1 line on their way to the Internet.

The business communications channel typically consists of a leased digital line (a T1 or fractional T1 line) connected to the ISP. The T1 line connects to one computer on the Local Area Network (LAN) called the router. The router is able to direct signals to and from all computers on the network to the ISP along the T1 line. In this manner all users achieve an Internet connection by sharing a single line. You will probably never see the router or T1 line since they are typically locked away in a wiring closet. The following table summarizes this information.

Component	From Home	From an Organization
Communications Channel	Regular telephone line	Fractional T1 line connected to a Frame Relay Network
Communications Hardware	Modem	Local Area Network (LAN) and a router
Communications Software	Dialer; Web browser	LAN operating system and a Web browser
Computer (recommended specs— you can get by with less)	200 MHz Pentium II 32 MB RAM 2 GB Hard drive Sound card Speakers (or similarly equipped Macintosh)	Same

For home use, most ISP's charge monthly flat rate billing with unlimited access. The charge now averages about $15 to $20 per month and is falling fast. Want some advice? Find someone who is happy with their service and follow their lead. Saving $2 per month is not worth the aggravation of bad service.

It's always a good idea to know what questions to ask. Consider the following points when you're shopping for an ISP.

Does the ISP have a local number for your area? You need to call the provider each time you access the Internet. Paying a toll call every time you do so will cost you a ton of money if you use the Internet regularly.

Can the system handle a large number of simultaneous connections? Ask them how many users they can handle at one time and how many subscribers they have. Although they may have a reasonable price and a local number, it doesn't mean much if you can't get on to use it. If after you subscribe you find that you are never able to connect or that the only available access is late at night or early in the morning, then find a new ISP.

Do they offer SLIP/PPP connections? This is the type of connection that you'll need if you want to use a graphical browser like Navigator or Internet Explorer. Today, PPP connections have become the standard. Some ISP's offer only shell accounts, which require you to type in each command as you would with DOS. It is somewhat like driving a horse and buggy when everyone else has an automobile.

Is monthly subscription fee reasonable? Cheapest is not always best. Added features and staffing support are important points to consider when choosing a service. Some ISP's offer you unlimited monthly connection time at a flat fee, and others offer you a per-hour fee with additional hours costing extra. You will need to estimate your expected usage and purchase accordingly. Ask if there is a fee to upgrade your service if you find that you need more time. If you have a roommate, then consider upgrading the service and splitting the cost. This may actually save you money.

Does your ISP include the Internet browser software in the price? You'll find that not all do. Most ISP's have an agreement with either Netscape or Microsoft to bundle their browser software. Fortunately, both browsers can be downloaded for free on the Internet. The provided software may also be partially configured to work on the ISP's system, so you'll be much farther along by using it and the technicians will be better able to help you with a problem.

Is the ISP a regional or local company? This may not be important to everyone, but some of you may go home during holidays or travel far and wide during vacations, and your destinations may be quite far from campus. If the ISP covers a wide enough area, then you can still check your e-mail and cruise the Net when you are away from school.

Do they have a help line in case you need technical assistance to set up your connection? Call the help line before you subscribe and make sure you get a real person. Although you may be asked to leave your name and number, you should expect to get a return call within 24 hours. If they don't return your call within this time period, then the service is probably understaffed or poorly managed.

Does the ISP offer both newsgroup and e-mail access in addition to a connection to the Web? This is usually standard, but there are always exceptions. It's better to ask up front.

Does it cost you extra for additional e-mail addresses? If you have a roommate, then you may find that it is more affordable to split the cost of a subscription and pay for an additional e-mail account.

Will your ISP add newsgroups at your request? Most ISP's subscribe to a small fraction of the available newsgroups, and you may find that they don't include some of the basic, business-oriented groups that your instructors may recommend. It shouldn't cost anything for the ISP to add these groups to their list.

Does the ISP offer you space for your own Web page? Often, one of the features offered in the basic package is the option of constructing and posting your own page. The ISP usually sets a memory usage limit that affects the total size of the page and its traffic flow (that is, the number of people viewing the site).

The most important thing to remember when using an ISP is to expect courteous and prompt service. If you don't like what you are paying for, then cancel and go somewhere else. There are plenty of competitors willing to offer you better service.

What sort of ISP should a business consider?

Business users pay significantly more per month since they connect at a higher speed. As prices for Internet connections for businesses are also in free fall, it makes little sense to enter into contracts for longer than one year. Since the price increases with the speed of the connection, it is best to buy less bandwidth initially as long as you can increase speed in the future without significant upgrade penalties. Advice for businesses? Hire a reputable management team to design your network, negotiate with vendors, and see the project through to completion. This way when something goes wrong (and it always does) it is the management team's problem and not yours.

Why are there mistakes in this book?

They changed their Web site, that's why! Home pages change. This will happen to you somewhere in this book. So, what should you do?

One thing that might help is to understand the path system used in Web page naming. Suppose you visit the site: **www.cc.gatech.edu/gvu/user_surveys**. The first part (**www.cc.gatech.edu**) identifies the host computer at that site. All pages at the site are contained in folders (subdirectories) of the host computer. For example, suppose the information you need is in the gvu/user_surveys folder. Fortunately, you rarely need to know in which subdirectory the information you are searching for is contained. A well-designed site will have a home page on the host computer at the top level (**www.cc.gatech.edu**) with links to all the pages on the site. So if **www.cc.gatech.edu/gvu/user_surveys** is not bringing you the information that you require, then simply back up to **www.cc.gatech.edu** and work your way down by following the links.

Another thing to remember is that there are many sources for some types of information. If something changes, try using search engines to find another source that will answer your questions. This step will really increase your surfing skills.

By the way, being able to change a home page is good. Content providers can continually update their pages and change graphics to make them more useful, without bearing the heavy costs of printed materials. They can experiment with new ideas at low cost and keep things fresh so consumers will be enticed to return.

How do I know that an online source is credible?

Just because information is on the Internet doesn't mean that it's complete, accurate, or objective. Before you use data from any online source, ask:

- What do you know about the source? When in doubt, seek out online sources that have a reputation for reliability. Many Web sites are sponsored by well-known organizations, such as major newspapers, that have earned a reputation for integrity. On the other hand, some Web sites don't even identify their sponsors. So be wary if the source is completely unfamiliar or has a questionable reputation.
- Does the source seem biased? Think about whether the source is likely to have a definite point of view on certain issues. For example, when you browse the Web site of the American Association of Retired Persons, bear in mind that the information is likely to reflect that group's role as an advocate for people over 50 years old. Knowing the organization's purpose and viewpoint can help you interpret any information you use from that source.
- What is the original source of the information? In many cases, Web sites and databases draw their information from other sources, such as government studies. If the original source is noted, take time to evaluate its reputation and potential for bias before you use the data. If no original source is indicated, approach the data with caution.
- Can you verify the source's information? Before you use information from an online source, try to find another source to verify the data. You can use a search tool such as Infoseek or Metacrawler to scan the Internet for the same kind of data provided by at least one other reliable source. The ability to confirm information serves as a valuable check on the data's accuracy—and the accuracy of its source.
- Does the source's information seem reasonable to you? As a final check on any online source, use your judgment to evaluate the data and the conclusions. Given the other facts you have uncovered on the subject, does this source's information seem unreasonable or out of line? If so, it's time to find a better source.

How does plagiarism apply to information from online sources?

Online research is so convenient that you may be tempted simply to copy material from an Internet source and paste it intact within your document. However, unless your sources are properly documented, you will be plagiarizing. Whether you're working on a term paper or researching a business report, you should cite your source when you (1) quote word-for-word, (2) closely paraphrase, or (3) repeat a series of phrases from documents posted on the Internet. This includes news articles, books or excerpts, surveys, speeches, transcripts of online discussions, manuals, and any material on Web pages sponsored by individuals, corporations, schools, nonprofit groups, or government agencies. When in doubt, you can avoid even the hint of plagiarism by fully document your sources.

So where do I go for more information?

Well, why not jump right onto the net? Use the following Internet addresses to research the right browser for you. Keep in mind that if the complete Internet address is not entered correctly you will not connect to that site. Internet addresses are case-sensitive so be sure to type them exactly as indicated.

Netscape
   http://www.netscape.com
Microsoft
   http://www.microsoft.com

Now, with your computer, modem, and browser, you're only one step away. Use the following Internet addresses to research the right ISP for you. You might want to consider the questions outlined earlier.

Choosing An Internet Provider
    http://tcp.ca/Dec95/Commtalk_ToC.html
Internet Access Provider Guide
    http://www.liii.com/~dhjordan/students/docs/welcome.htm
Choosing the Internet Service Provider Netscape
    http://home.netscape.com/assist/isp_select/index.html

It is always nice to have an independent opinion. Read what the critics have to say. Stop by the following Internet addresses, and visit the largest publishers of computer-related magazines. Altogether, these companies print nearly 50 different popular periodicals about computers and the Internet. Search their databases for articles that will help you decide. You can read the articles online.

CMP Media Inc.'s (Publisher of Windows Magazine and others)
    http://www.techweb.com/info/publications/publications.html
Ziff Davis (Publisher of PC Magazine, MacUser, and others)
    http://www5.zdnet.com/findit/search.html

Chapter 2
Up and Running: The Search is On

Let's look now at how to use the browser for navigating the Internet. First we discuss basic navigation techniques. Then we introduce you to how to conduct searches on the Internet.

Cruising the Net

Although the Internet may seem large and disorganized, finding your way around is no harder then finding your way to a friend's house. Information on the Internet has an address just as your friend does. Most browsers allow you to type in an address and access information from, or "go to," a particular document.

Let's take a look at how to enter an address using the Web browser Netscape Navigator, shown in Figure 2.1. Start by finding the text entry box, to the right of the words *Netsite*. (Sometimes the words *Location* or *Go to* appear instead.) If you have Navigator, type in the address and press the return button on your keyboard. Be sure to type in the address accurately. Even one mistake will prevent you from making the connection you want.

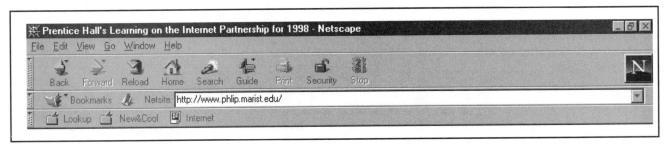

Figure 2.1. The tool bar for Netscape Navigator offers basic navigation features such as Back, Forward, and Home. You will find everything you'll need to perform simple navigation around the Internet.

Now take a look at the row of icons directly above the text box. This is known as the *Navigation Tool Bar*. Clicking on an individual icon causes the computer to execute the command noted below the icon.

How do each of these commands help you to navigate the Internet? In Figure 2.1, find the button labeled *Back*—it's at the far left. By clicking on this button you can return to the Web page you just visited. If you have gone to many Web pages, you can use the *Back* button repeatedly to return to your starting point.

Now find the *Home* button. By selecting this button, you will immediately return to the home page configured for your browser. When you first begin using your browser, it will be set to a page determined by the company that created it. At some point you may want to change your home page or even create your own. But for now, remember that you can always go home.

Two other buttons common to most browsers are *Stop* and *Reload*. The Stop button stops your computer from downloading information from the address that you have just asked for. *Reload* needs just a bit more explanation. As you explore more of the Internet, you'll realize that complete pages don't show up in your browser window instantly. Instead, different types of elements (pictures, icons, text, animations, and so on) appear over time as they are moved from the server to your browser. Occasionally, you'll notice that a page loads without some of these elements. This is often caused by an error in the transmission. Use the *Reload* button to request a new copy of the page.

You don't always have to know the address of a page to view that page. The wonderful thing about the Web is that you can access (navigate) pages through the use of *hyperlinks*. You will notice that hyperlinks are often colored words (typically blue) on a Web page. Images may also be hyperlinks. Click your mouse on the desired hyperlink, and you will travel to a new Web page, just as you would if you typed in an address (see Figure 2.2).

Figure 2.2 Hyperlinks can be words or images. Note that the cursor, on the image, is now a hand, indicating that it is a hyperlink.

The author of a Web page can connect *one* image to *many* different places. This type of hyperlink is sometimes called a *clickable map*, or *image map*. For example, think of a Web page with a map of the United States. For any place you might want more information on, just point your mouse to it and click! You are linked to another location with more details on that particular part of the country. Go ahead and try it for yourself by visiting the sites in the following box.

Here are two addresses that use clickable maps. The second is one of the most popular law sites maintained by the TV network, Court TV.

> City.Net Travel
> http://city.net/countries/united_states/
> U.S. Census Bureau
> http://www.census.gov/datamap/www/

Note that clickable maps do not necessarily need to be in a format of a traditional "map." The Court TV site is a good example. Also note that not all browsers support clickable maps. However, most good Web authors will provide conventional hyperlinks to related sites in addition to the clickable map.

Some Web pages contain *forms*. A form is generally a request for information, which you may respond to by clicking with your mouse or typing an answer. Forms can be used to survey users, answer questions, or make requests. If you'd like to see a Web page that uses forms, you might want to visit a college or university admissions office site. Those sites often use forms to develop contacts with prospective students. One example is the University of Minnesota's Admissions Office site.

> The University of Minnesota Admissions Office
> http://admissions.tc.umn.edu/info/mailA.html

Return Visit

Now that you've found some *really* interesting pages, how do you find them again a day or a week later without going through the same hassle? Your browser provides a way to mark a site so you can quickly return to it. Netscape calls this feature *Bookmarks* (see Figure 2.3), and Microsoft calls this feature *Favorites*. With this feature you can compile a list of pages you frequently visit. When you wish to return to one of these pages, you simply select it from the list by clicking on it with your mouse. You will jump directly to the site.

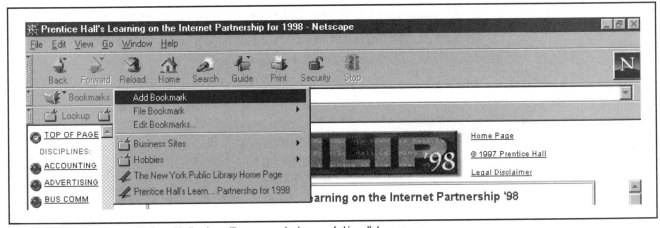

Figure 2.3. As bookmarks are added to this list they will appear at the bottom of this pull-down menu.

Here is an address to get your bookmark collection started. Try this: http://www.hotwired.com . It's the online version of Wired Magazine and an interesting site. If you have Netscape, select *Add Bookmark* from the *Bookmarks* menu (see Figure 2.3). Later on, if you use your mouse to select the *Bookmarks* menu, you'll see that *Hotwired* is just a jump away. You don't have to memorize the address or haphazardly jump around until you find it again.

As you begin to accumulate more sites, you'll notice how cluttered and disorganized your list can become. Most browsers allow you to organize bookmarks as you desire. Let's assume you have a rich list of business-related bookmarks, and you want to put them in order. From the *Bookmarks* menu, select *Edit Bookmarks* and then select *File*. From this menu, select *New Folder*. You will then be prompted to type in a name and description(optional) for your new folder. Perhaps you want to add a folder for marketing. Type *Marketing*, then click OK. You then just click on whatever addresses you want to add in this folder and drag them to that folder name.

To view what is in a particular folder, just click on *Bookmarks* and place the cursor on the folder name. A menu will pop up with a list of the bookmarks you've stored there.

For Web sites that you access on a regular basis, you can create a button (hyperlink) on the Personal Toolbar by just clicking on the icon to the right of *Bookmarks* and dragging it to the *Personal Toolbar*. You have to be visiting the Web site at the time to create this link.

Go and History

If you've been working along with this guide and your browser at the same time, you've probably been to many places on the Web. If you are moving back and forth between your selections, you are probably using the *Forward* and *Back* buttons on the browser toolbar. But what if you want to go back fifteen jumps? Do you press the *Back* button fifteen times? Well, that works, but it is a little slow. You might want to try a different approach, which allows you to jump rapidly to any of the places you've visited along your path of travel. In Navigator, select the *Go* menu. You'll see a list of all of the places you've visited on your journey. Select the appropriate site, and away you go. You might also use *History*, which appears under the *Windows* menu. You'll open a new window listing the names and the addresses for all of the places you've been to recently. Other browsers have similar features.

Because the lists compiled under *Go* and *History* begin anew each time you start your browser, you should still use *Bookmarks* when you find something interesting.

Asking for Directions

The Internet is truly vast. It contains plenty of valuable information, but it's not always easy to find what you need. To help you find your way, however, a number of easy-to-use tools are available for free. With practice, these tools will help you develop better information-finding skills. Our next section offers a look at how to streamline your journeys through the Net.

Search Strategies

Let's focus now on search techniques that will help you find the information you need on the Web. Some of the search techniques are very basic. Others take some time to master. It is worth learning all these search techniques because they will increase your Net research efficiency and effectiveness.

We turn to Open Text and Subject Tree searches. Open text searches scan the Web looking for a word or group of words you have entered as your search string. The search engine then lists links to pages on the Web that it determines are most relevant to your search string. A page with more matches is considered more likely to be relevant.

A subject tree search takes a different approach. A subject tree is a catalog of a great number of pages on the Web, neatly organized by category, sub-category, sub-sub-category, and so on. For example, suppose you wanted to look into the economics of selling athletic wear. You could follow any number of paths, and we'll give you one example here that you could find with Yahoo!, which we'll explain soon:

Business ⇒ Companies ⇒ Apparel ⇒ Athletic Wear ⇒ Footwear ⇒ Brand Names ⇒ Nike

There you are. Along the way, as you read through the various sub-categories, you may develop new ideas for what information you want to find and how you'll get to it. Users navigate down through the subject tree until they reach a link pointing to a page that looks relevant. There is more work involved in a subject tree search than in an open text search, but the results are often worth the effort. We generally recommend beginning with a subject tree search for three reasons. First, people — not robot programs — compile subject trees, and these people cut out links that are useless. Second, subject trees help orient your search by showing you which sites fall into the same category. This grouping may lead you to discover sources of information that you had not considered. Third, the premier subject tree index, Yahoo!, is very good.

Indeed Yahoo! is actually a bit of a hybrid between subject tree and open text searches. In addition to offering the ability to drill down manually, there is also a search feature on Yahoo! that shows you all categories matching your search term. Furthermore, after showing you its own matches, Yahoo! also offers you the option of transferring your search to AltaVista (another, more detailed search engine) for even more matches.

Why so many search engines?

Let's consider Yahoo! (a subject tree) and AltaVista (open text search). A couple of graduate school dropouts from Stanford created Yahoo!. AltaVista has corporate roots: Digital Equipment started It. The two engines have a unique relationship since Yahoo! will pass along an open text search to AltaVista for processing. So why use anything else? Well, like all products in the service sector, each search engine has unique features. Some catalog a greater percentage of the Web, some are faster, some have more advanced search features, some are geared toward a specialized area of information, and some will translate your words into a concept and then search for the concept. There are even meta search engines that simultaneously feed your query to multiple search engines for processing! The best approach is to learn how to use one or two search engines well and then generalize your knowledge to other search engines as needed.

Subject Tree Index

A subject tree, as we have pointed out, is an index to the World Wide Web organized by categories and sub-categories. The most comprehensive subject tree index on the Web is Yahoo!. Try it yourself! To start Yahoo! you need first to launch your Web browser. This will probably be either Microsoft's Internet Explorer or Netscape Navigator which looks like this:

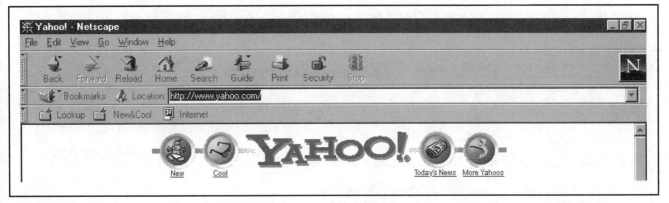

Figure 2.4   Netscape Navigator is one of the most widely used Web browsers available today.

To get to Yahoo!'s site you type: **www.yahoo.com** in the Address or Location line of your browser and then press the return key.   Some of the top level Yahoo! categories appear below:

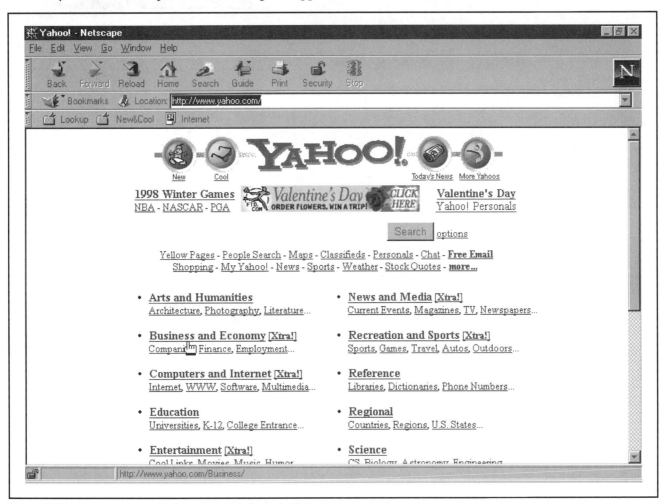

Figure 2.5   Yahoo is the most comprehensive subject tree index on the Web.

To explore the business category more in depth you click on <u>Business and Economy</u>. This brings up a list of all of the business and economics sub-categories, which looks like this:

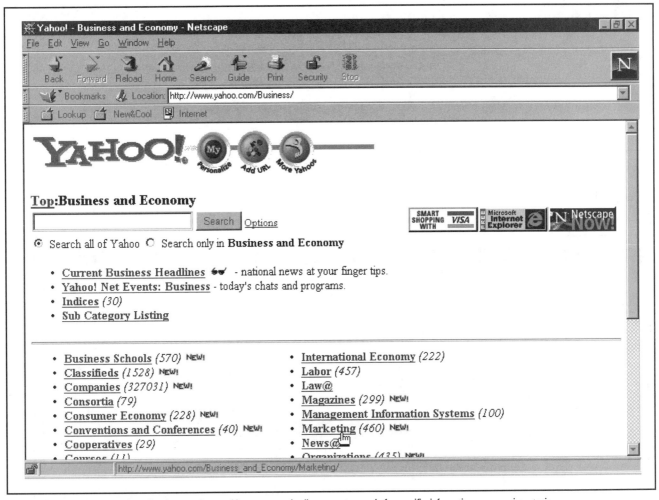

Figure 2.6 By digging down through sub-categories, a subject tree search allows you to search for specific information on any given topic.

Yahoo! boldfaces sub-categories as well as indicating the number of entries in parentheses. For example we know that the Marketing sub-category contains 460 entries, some of which are relatively new. To explore the marketing category more in depth you click on <u>Marketing</u> and you will see:

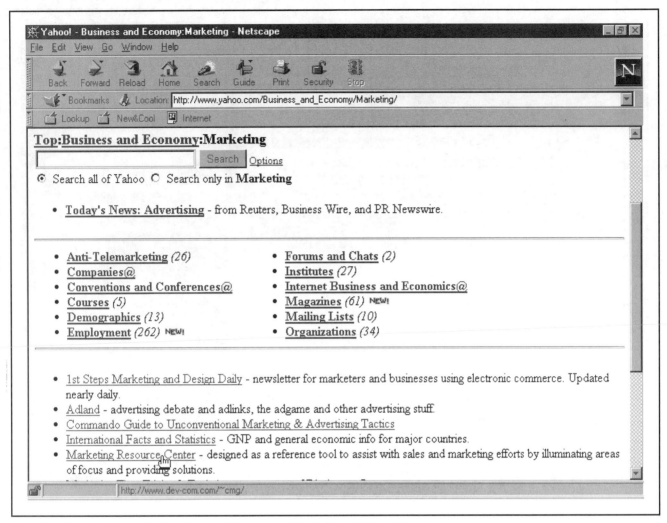

Figure 2.7   Below the sub-categories, Yahoo! lists direct links to other Web sites that might be of interest to you.

At this level we see that there are further sub-categories such as <u>Demographics</u>, <u>Employment</u>, and <u>Organizations</u>. Below these sub-categories we also see entries that are direct links to marketing-related sites on the Internet. For example, by scrolling down and clicking on Marketing Resource Center we are lead directly to a wealth of information along with hyperlinks to other marketing related sites (see Figure 2.8).

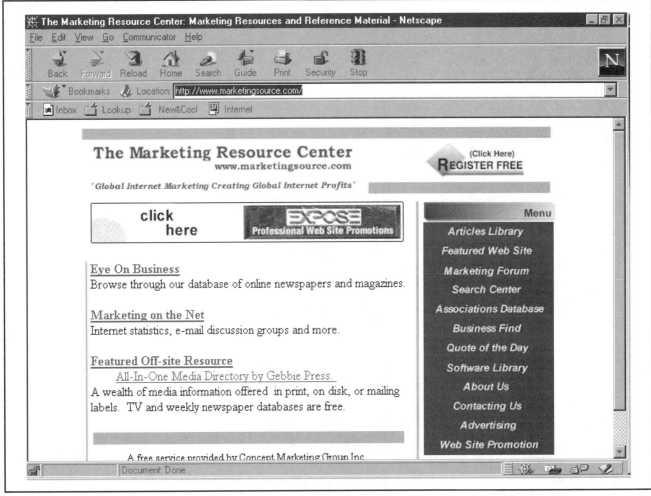

Figure 2.8 The Marketing Resource Center page is one step on an infinite path of hyperlink connections.

Note how for the first time the address has changed so that we are no longer on Yahoo!'s site. We have followed a link off of Yahoo!'s index to another site somewhere else in the world.

Your Turn

Using the Yahoo! subject tree index, locate the site for Advertising Age. Begin at the top level and drill down until a direct link is found.

How many levels did you have to drill down to reach the site?
What other links at the final level look like they might be worth exploring?

Open Text Search

An open text search is a keyword search through the entire Web. All pages matching the keywords are returned by the search engine and then ranked in order of relevance. Generally, pages containing the keywords the greatest number of times are given a higher relevance rating. Since thousands of documents can contain the same keywords it is important for you to be as specific as possible in your search.

Yahoo! incorporates open text searching in two ways (see Figure 2.9). First, it allows you to search the entire Yahoo! site when you enter a term in the search box and then press the search button. For example, if we enter Nike in the search box, we get the following results:

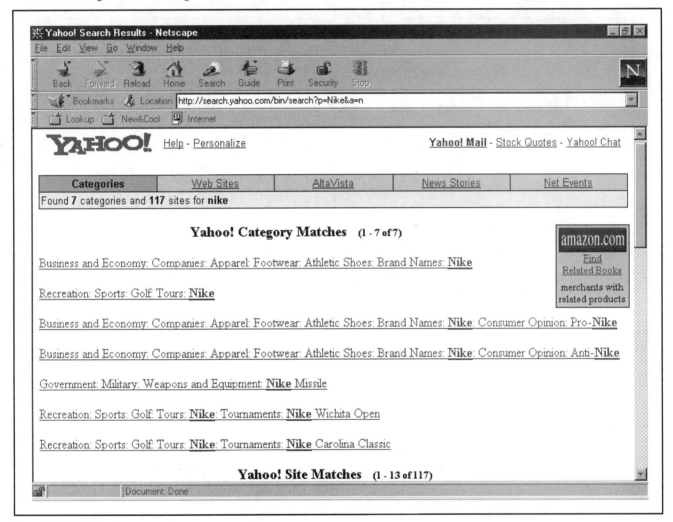

Figure 2.9 Yahoo! also allows you to do an open text search.

This tells us that Yahoo! has seven categories under which Nike is listed. Additionally, it has categorized links to 117 different sites that contain information about the company.

Second, Yahoo! allows us to transfer our search to AltaVista if none of the links provided are useful (see Figure 2.10).

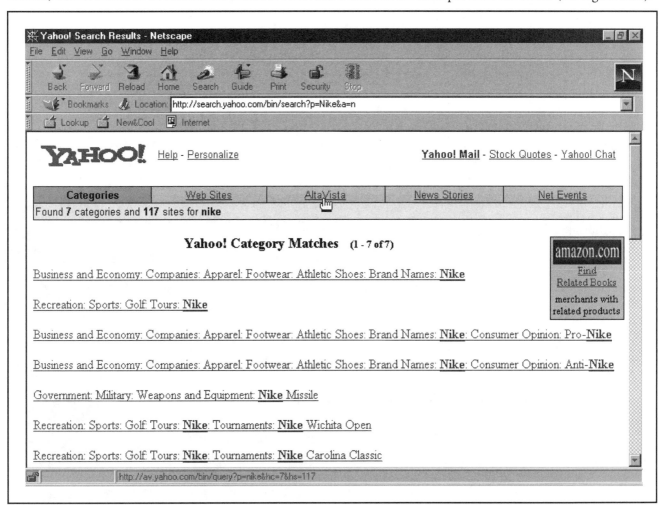

Figure 2.10 If the result of your Yahoo! search is insufficient, additional search results are just a click away with Yahoo's! direct link to AltaVista.

By clicking on the AltaVista item our search is transferred to AltaVista and the results look like this:

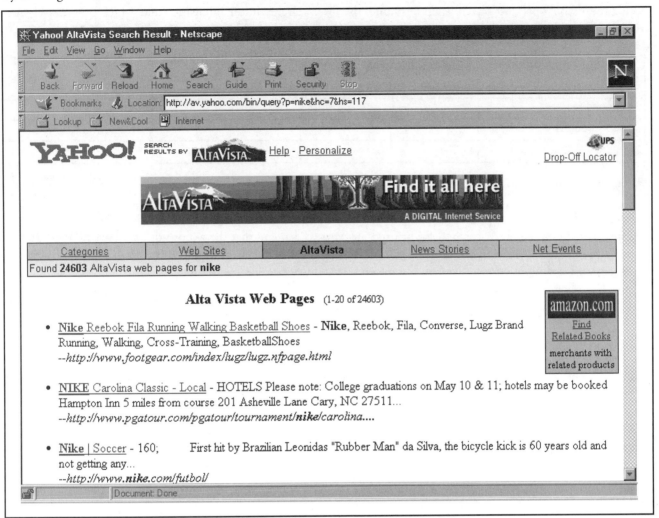

Figure 2.11 AltaVista has come up with a much greater number of related Web sites with an open text search, but more is not always better. If you know what you are looking for, it would be more productive to fine tune your results through a category search. (DIGITAL, AltaVista and the AltaVista logo are trademarks or service marks of Digital Equipment Corporation. Used in permission.)

Note that AltaVista has found 24,603 Web pages that mention Nike. The first 20 matches are displayed on the page. The first one shown is supposed to be the most relevant. But is it? Can you begin to see why we like you to start with Yahoo!?

Your Turn

Using the Yahoo! open text search feature, conduct the three searches in the following table, which progressively narrow down a subject. Record the number of matches given with each search string.

Keywords Searched for	Number of Yahoo! category matches	Number of Yahoo! site matches	Number of AltaVista pages
coupons			
food coupons			
grocery food coupons			

What conclusions can you draw from this experiment?

Sometimes the keywords appear on the same page but with hundreds of words separating them. This results in a list of irrelevant sites. Open text searches also incorporate ways to demand that the words not only have to appear on the same page but also must be right next to one another. The easiest way to accomplish this is to put the words that must appear together in quotes. The best way to understand this point is to try it out.

Try an open text search for northeast economic forecast.

How relevant are your search results?

Now try an open text search for northeast "economic forecast"

How relevant is the information returned? Propose an explanation for the difference in results.

Knowing which words to put in quotes is not always obvious since there are times when the keywords never appear right next to each other. Try an open text search for "northeast economic forecast"

Did you get any results?

We hope you're starting to feel comfortable traveling the Net. We're going to move now to advanced search techniques.

Advanced Search

Sometimes a simple search turns up rather strange results. In the basic search exercise we saw how quotes could be helpful in limiting the results to useful information. We now introduce some powerful operators that will help you save tremendous amounts of time when searching the Web.

The basic search exercise introduced the Yahoo! search engine. When you performed an open text search in that exercise, the engine first searched the Yahoo! subject tree, showed you Yahoo!'s results, and then passed along the search to AltaVista and showed you AltaVista's results. The Yahoo! subject tree contains all of the pages that the Yahoo! editors have had time to categorize. And while they have categorized a lot, the Yahoo! subject tree is far from complete. By contrast, AltaVista uses a robot program to search the Web and index documents by keywords. AltaVista's robots work tirelessly day and night, and so they are able to visit millions of pages on the Web and index all the keywords that they find. We present AltaVista in this exercise because it complements Yahoo! and because it is quite fast.

Pluses and Minuses

To search the Web most effectively means being able to specify what you want and what you don't want. In AltaVista a plus means that you want the word to appear on a Web page, and a minus means that you don't. So +inflation -currency gives you all sites that have inflation but no currency. Conversely, -inflation +currency gives you all sites that have no inflation but lots on currency. Ready? Start up AltaVista by entering its address in your Web browser—www.altavista.digital.com. You should see a welcome page similar to this:

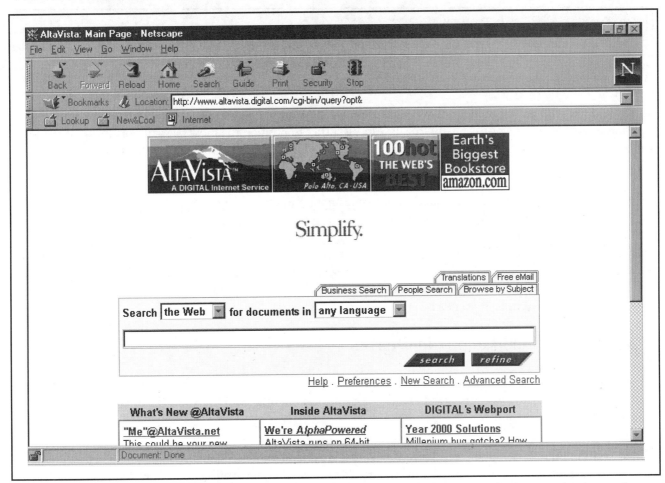

Figure 2.12 AltaVista's home page allows you to refine your open text search on the Web. (DIGITAL, AltaVista and the AltaVista logo are trademarks or service marks of Digital Equipment Corporation. Used in permission.)

Your Turn

You now enter a search string in the box and then click the button. Let's try our inflation and currency example. Be sure to include a space between the words, or AltaVista will think you are searching for one long word.

You Type	It Means
+inflation -currency	Find all pages that have information on inflation but not currency

About how many documents were returned by the query?

Are you going to read them all? We didn't think so. Now try the second example.

You Type	It Means
-inflation +currency	Find all pages that do not cover inflation but have information on currency

About how many documents were returned by the query?

As you can see, with tens of millions of Web sites covered, AltaVista is going to find a lot of references. Some will be right on target, but most won't be useful to you. AltaVista tries to position the most relevant documents at the top of the list. So how does it determine what's relevant? Generally, AltaVista uses the following criteria to rank a document's relevance:
- the query words or phrases are found in the first few words of the document
- the query words or phrases are found close to one another in the document
- the document contains more than one instance of the query word or phrase

Unfortunately, unscrupulous Web site designers have caught on to these conventions, and some sites overpopulate their sites with keywords so that they appear first in the listings. For example, we once came across a car dealer that repeated Toyota Toyota Toyota… in order to earn a higher relevance rating and thus attract surfers looking for a Toyota site. To filter out these false relevant ratings the better search engines might require, for example, that duplicate instances of keywords be separated by at least seven words.

Keep it Together; Keep it in Quotes

As we said, AltaVista places pages higher on its search results list when the search words appear close together on the Web page. Sometimes you want the search words right next to each other with no words in between. To accomplish this we put the words in quotes.

Your Turn

Let's say we are interested in pages on Web marketing. We'll try typing the words with and without quotes.

You Type	It Means
Web marketing	Find all pages that have the words Web and marketing

About how many documents did the query find?

Now let's try it with the quotes to force the words to appear right next to each other.

You Type	It Means
"Web marketing"	Find all pages that have the words "Web" and "marketing" where those words right next to each other.

About how many documents did the query find?

Finally, we'll limit further to just those sites which mention the Nielsen Survey.

You Type	It Means
+"Web marketing" + "nielsen survey"	Find all pages that have the words Web and marketing where those words appear right next to each other. Those same sites must also have the words "nielsen" and "survey" right next to each other.

About how many documents did the query find?

You can get very specific!

WHEN IN DOUBT, lowercase

You may have noticed that in all of the examples above, we typed the search strings in lowercase letters, even when searching for a proper name such as Nielsen. The reason for this is that lowercase search strings match both lower and uppercase, but uppercase matches uppercase only. So, if some webmaster forgets to capitalize Nielsen, you'll still find that site.

A Star for the Wildcard

What if you are looking for information on European free trade zones? It is reasonable to assume that Europe free trade zones might also produce good results. Rather than run two searches – European free trade zones and Europe free trade zones — we can use the wildcard notation to match all words that start with Europe (that is, both Europe and European) by typing europe*.

Your Turn

Try the following example:

You Type	It Means
+europe* +"free trade zones"	Find all pages that have words that begin with europe. Those same pages must have the words "free trade zones" right next to each other

About how many documents were returned by the query?

Who is Linked to Us?

On the Web, more is better when it comes to site visitors: More visitors means more potential business. Visitors can link to a site in many ways:

1. by deducing or guessing a site name (for example, www.coca-cola.com)
2. by searching for the site using a search engine
3. by copying the address from an advertisement or other media
4. by following a "hot link" from another site

Coopers and Lybrand Consulting found that 39% of Web users learn about sites through other media, 44% through word-of-mouth, 32% through browsing, and 10% through "hot links" (source: **www.cyberatlas.com**).

We now focus on following a hot link from one site to another and begin with a fun exercise to determine which sites on the Web have a link to our site. The sincerest form of flattery on the Web is to put a free link on a home page to another site. The more folks that do it, the more traffic to the hot-linked site. What if we could find all the sites in the world that have a link to us? Well, we can.

Your Turn

Let's see which sites link to the American Airlines home page. The address for American Airlines is **www.americanair.com**. For the first query we want to find all sites that link to American Airlines, ordered by the number of times that they mention American Airlines on their home page.

You Type	It Means
link:www.americanair.com	Find all pages with a link to American Airlines

How many sites link to American Airlines?

Go to the first site on the list. Can you find the link to American Airlines? Where was it?

Interestingly, some search engines, but not AltaVista, actually use the number of links to a site to help compute its relevancy ranking. Not a bad idea since the Web community is effectively voting with its links.

Nevertheless, links from other sites are not always welcome. Ticketmaster sued Microsoft for providing a link to its site. The gripe? The Microsoft link did not point to the Ticketmaster home page but rather to a subpage. Ticketmaster wants to communicate with users through the "front door," perhaps so that they will see a full menu of products, promotions, and advertising.

Chapter 3
Getting Your Message Out in Style:
E-Mail and Other Enhancements

In chapter 2 we looked at how to conduct searches and find answers on the Internet. In other words, you've learned how to get information into your hands from the outside. But as valuable as that skill is, the flow of information has been only one way – to you. How do you move material from your computer to the outside world? Let's turn now to how e-mail works.

Staying in Touch with E-Mail

Navigator and most other browsers allow you to communicate through e-mail, newsgroups, and online interest groups. E-mail links are built into many Web pages and enable you to send correspondence directly to other people through the Internet.

E-mail is the electronic exchange of mail. Like Web browsers and Web servers, e-mail operates according to a Client-Server model. Think of the server as your mailbox, where messages addressed to you are stored until you pick them up. You use your mail client to retrieve them. Be careful about forgetting to pick up your mail. If you overload your mailbox, you may lose some pieces.

Getting to an e-mail server is easy. If you are at a campus that has provided you with Internet access, you should be able to apply for an e-mail account through your campus computer administration. Otherwise, you can apply for an e-mail account through an ISP. If you use an ISP to access the Internet, you probably have e-mail capabilities. To properly configure your browser for sending e-mail, you need to know your e-mail address and the name of your mail server.

Here's a little bit on why e-mail addresses look the way they do. The format of a typical e-mail address is as follows: NAME@HOST.DOMAIN. It is not necessary to have a full name for the NAME part of the address. In fact, some addresses use only numbers to represent an individual.

Here is an example of a typical e-mail address.

joan_waxman@prenhall.com

A typical e-mail address has three basic components:

user name	joan waxman
host server	prenhall
domain com	

The @ symbol always follows the user name. The host server appears next. The domain in the e-mail format, just like the domain of the URL format, indicates the user's affiliation. Notice that there are no spaces anywhere in an e-mail address.

Your campus computer administrator or your ISP will provide you with an e-mail account. This is the address you'll give to your friends and perhaps use as part of distance-learning classes. It will also be posted with any correspondence you send on the Internet.

To send and receive e-mail, you need to enter your e-mail address. Once again, in Netscape, move from *Edit* to *Preferences*. Now move to *Mail & Groups*. You'll see the label *Identity*. Click here and fill in the necessary information (Figure 3.1).

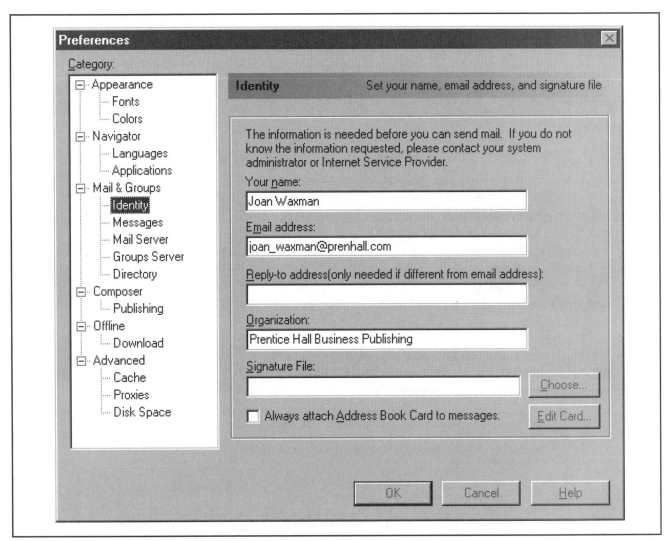

Figure 3.1. You identify yourself for e-mail communication at the Identity section within Preferences.

You need to set up your mail server. Under *Mail & Groups*, simply click on *Mail Server*. Note the directions above the boxes that you must fill in (see Figure 3.2). As they suggest, check with your system administrator or your ISP for the information that you need to enter on this screen.

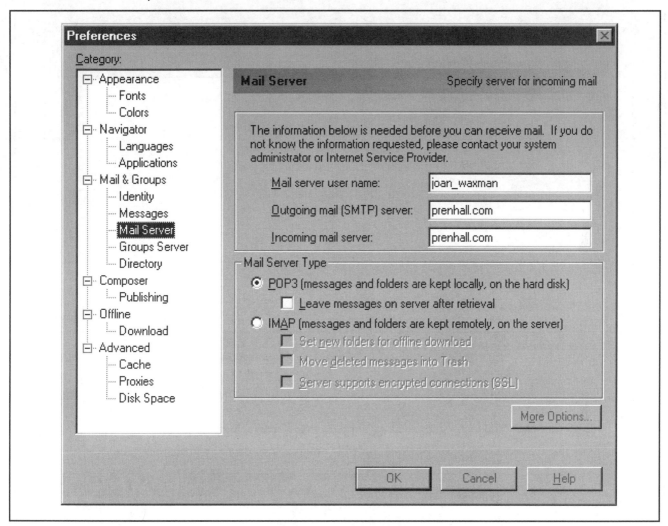

Figure 3.2 Before you can receive mail you must provide the information requested in Mail Server.

Now select the *Communicator* option from the menu bar and choose *Messenger Mailbox*. You could also open your mailbox simply by clicking on the *Mailbox* icon on the Communicator component bar, which is located in the lower right corner of your Netscape Communicator screen. Either way you will get a screen that looks like this:

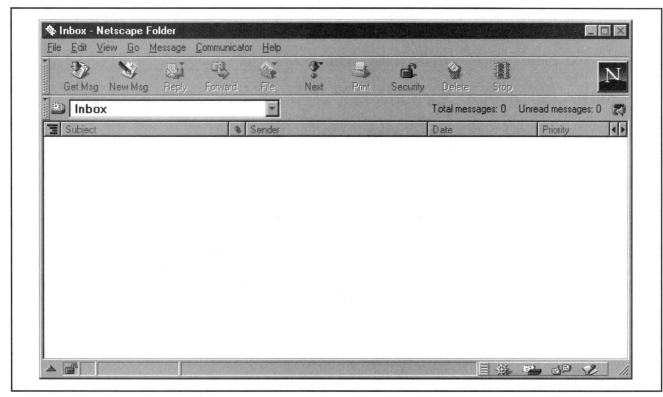

Figure 3.3 The toolbar makes it easy to quickly browse and reply to messages.

To retrieve your mail, select the *Get Msg* button. If you have mail, then it will appear below the *Locator Toolbar*. When you select a specific mail item you will see the contents displayed at the bottom of the window.

Maybe you know some people with an e-mail address. To send them a note click on the *New Msg* icon and a new window appears titled *Composition*. Here is where you will compose and edit the e-mail you send out.

Now that you've got the basics down, here is a site that provides more information on e-mail. It was written by Kaitlin Duck Sherwood.

A Beginner's Guide to Effective Email
http://www.webfoot.com/advice/estyle.html?Author

Newsgroups

Many browsers enable users to exchange ideas through newsgroups. A newsgroup is a set of people who connect to an address and participate in a specialized discussion. In some newsgroups, moderators post items for discussion and referee any electronic brawls that may arise. Others function without a moderator. All newsgroups provide a place where people can bring new ideas and perspectives to the table.

Where e-mail is sent and posted for a single person to read, news postings are sent to a common place for all participants to read and comment on. If e-mail is like the postal service, newsgroups are like coffee houses on open microphone night.

What is the purpose of the newsgroups if people just contribute ideas and comments to a mass discussion on a particular topic? Newsgroups are places where you can go and ask questions, get ideas, and learn about specific topics. Select a group that interests you, and see what you find.

The names of newsgroups usually describe their focus. There are several major newsgroup categories. Try the following.

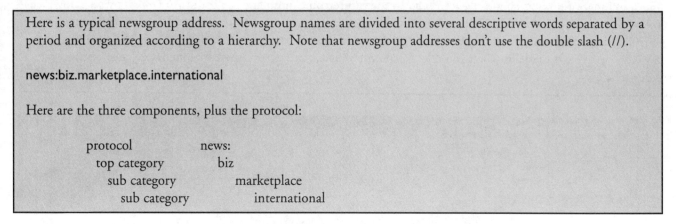

Here is a typical newsgroup address. Newsgroup names are divided into several descriptive words separated by a period and organized according to a hierarchy. Note that newsgroup addresses don't use the double slash (//).

news:biz.marketplace.international

Here are the three components, plus the protocol:

protocol	news:
top category	biz
sub category	marketplace
sub category	international

To configure your browser to connect to a newsgroup, you will need the name of the server computer that handles newsgroups. (Get this from the same people who gave you your e-mail server address.) To set your newsgroup information, select the *Edit* menu and then *Preferences* from the pull-down menu. Select *Groups Server* from the *Mail & Groups* category (see Figure 3.4).

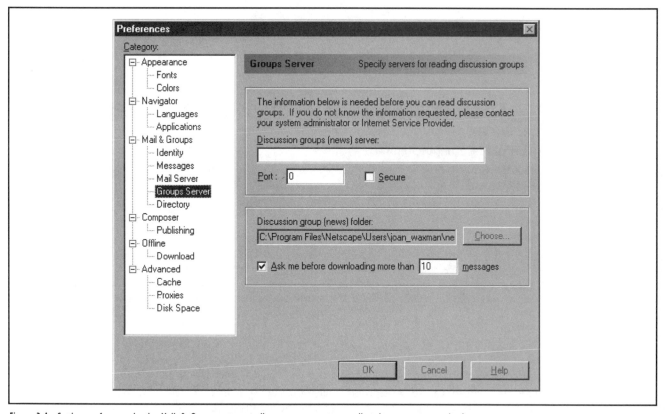

Figure 3.4 Setting preferences in the Mail & Groups category allows you access to e-mail and newsgroups on the Internet.

You may also click on *Collabra Discussion Groups* from the *Communicator* menu, at which point you will be prompted to enter server information. You may find that you can't access some newsgroups. Check to make sure your ISP subscribes to these. If not, it will usually do so if you make a request.

To view a list of newsgroups you can select *Subscribe* from the toolbar and choose *All Groups*. If this is your first time searching for groups, choose *New Groups*. In the future you can update the list in *All Groups* by selecting *New Groups* and clicking on *Get New*. You can subscribe to specific groups by checking them off. Click OK when you are finished making your selections. You will then see the selected groups listed in the *Netscape Message Center* window (see Figure 3.5). Finally, when you select a specific article, you will see the contents displayed in the news reader window.

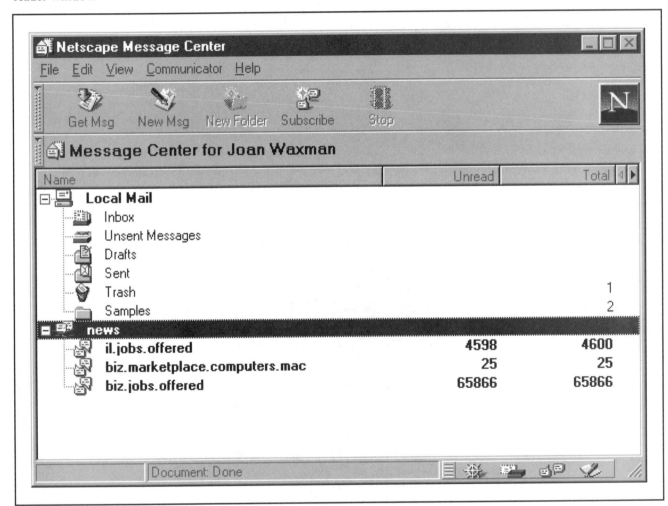

Figure 3.5 Netscape Message Center lists each group you subscribe to. Just click on a newsgroup to view the list of messages.

Chat

This is yet another avenue for communication. It is probably the one you'll choose if you like to gab. Unlike e-mail and newsgroups, which require you to wait for a response, chat rooms are real-time. This means that you are conversing and observing conversations as they happen. Chat rooms are easily accessible through search engines, such as

Yahoo! and Excite, and do not require any special browser configuration. As with newsgroups, it is best to observe the interactions of several chat rooms and read the new-user information before you jump in. Some rooms can be excessive and vulgar, but many are frequented by polite people with a genuine desire to communicate honestly. Just like newsgroups, chat rooms are organized by topic, and you can usually anticipate the conversation by the name of the group.

Just to get you started, here are a few Web-based chat groups.

WebChat Broadcasting System
http://webchat5.wbs.net/
Jammin's ChatPlanet Chat Room!
http://www.jammin.com/livechat.html
Matt's PaleoChat Room
http://www.pitt.edu/~mattf/PaleoChat.html

Read the instructions and ask for help if you get confused.

Unlike e-mail and newsgroups, you will be frequently asked to log-in or register before you can chat. Often you'll even be given a password. Always read the rules for participating and ask for help if you don't understand something. The participants are generally very helpful. In chat rooms you will typically use a "handle," or pseudonym, when you post a message. Some people find chat rooms to be more entertaining than educational, but decide for yourself.

Mailing Lists

Electronic mailing lists, also called listservs, allow participants to post and read e-mail messages in a running discussion about a special interest topic. Some listservs are moderated, with a discussion leader screening every message before sending it to everyone on the list. However, in unmoderated listservs, no one screens the messages before they are sent out. You must subscribe to a listserv in order to participate; then, if you want to remove your name from the discussion list, you have to unsubscribe. Later in this guide, you will read about a variety of listservs that cover business-related topics.

Language for the Road

A few words of caution. Unlike face-to-face conversations between people, electronic exchanges restrict your ability to use vocal inflections, facial expression, and body language while communicating. (These options aren't easily digitized and transmitted across the wires unless you have an Internet telephone or video conference capability. These are available if you have a powerful system, but for most of us they are not practical.) You will need to practice the way you communicate electronically and be patient when someone misinterprets something you've "said." For example, suppose you tell a joke. Because the reader gets only the text, she may think that you are serious and take offense. Computer hacks learned about this problem a long time ago and developed several solutions. They are called smileys. You'll have to turn your head side-ways to view them:

:-)	This is a happy face
;-)	This is a wink.
:-(	This is a sad face.
:-[	This is a really sad face.

Because you eventually will get tired of typing all of the things you have to say, several sets of initials are commonly used. Here are but a few:

BTW   By The Way
IMHO   In My Humble Opinion
FYI   For Your Information
FAQ   Frequently Asked Question

Like any other culture, the Internet has borrowed some common words but use them in a context you might not normally expect. Here are two that you'll commonly see:

Flame   The act of yelling, insulting, or degrading a person. You can expect to get flamed if you don't follow certain basic rules of netiquette (etiquette of the Net).

Spam   The act of posting a comment, message, or advertisement to multiple newsgroups when the note doesn't pertain to them all. It is the Internet equivalent of sending junk mail.

These are a few Web resources that you will definitely want to read when you begin communicating online. They are very helpful and at times even pretty funny. Enjoy!

E-Mail Etiquette
http://www.iwillfollow.com/email.htm
The Net: User Guidelines and Netiquette By Arlene H. Rinaldi
http://rs6000.adm.fau.edu/rinaldi/net/index.htm
Electronic Frontier Foundation's Unofficial Smiley Dictionary
http://www.eff.org/papers/eegtti/eeg_286.html

There's Always Room to Improve

In early Web history, travel was pretty basic. The browser was a piece of software that acted as a totally self-contained vehicle. When you hooked it up, it contained everything you needed to cruise the Net. But as the Web has grown larger, people have developed new formats for presenting information on the Web. Digital video, audio, animations, interactive games, and 3D worlds are currently very common on the Internet. Eventually, as people demand more functionality from the Internet, new and richer formats will be developed. To cope with this continuing change, Netscape has developed a way to add functionality without overloading the basic browser design.

Helpers and Plug-ins

Early Web pages included only text and images. They were much like brochures with the ability to hyperlink to other pages. As Web pages grew more sophisticated, so did the format in which their images were presented. The browser was no longer enough to display these images. People had to turn to an external program – that is, a program outside the browser – to display these images. Such an outside program is called a helper application. Some developers decided to eliminate the helper application by bringing it inside the browser software. The result is called a plug-in. A plug-in is any program added to the internal workings of a browser. For example, if you want to listen to music on the Internet, you can install a plug-in that allows the browser to understand the audio format.

Netscape was critical to the development of many plug-ins, and this company is still the place to turn when you want one. An important point: Adding plug-ins to your browser will increase its requirement for memory (RAM). If you go overboard with the plug-ins, your browser might stop working. Add only the plug-ins that you're going to use regularly.

These addresses will take you to the place where you can download the plug-ins to your computer. These developers also provide a very good description of how to install them and make them work for you.

RealAudio by Progressive Networks
http://get.real.com/products/player/download.html
Shockwave by MacroMedia
http://www.macromedia.com/shockwave/download/
QuickTime by Apple
http://www.quicktime.apple.com/sw/

Once you've lived a little and added a plug-in or two (or too many), you can get a list of the ones you've installed right from your browser. Select the *Help* menu and then choose *About Plug-ins*. The browser window will then present a list of all of your installed plug-ins. If you click on the link at the top of the page, you will also be able to connect directly to Netscape's master plug-in page.

JavaScript and Java

As it turned out, helpers and plug-ins weren't enough. Web developers wanted even more — <u>more</u> flexibility, <u>more</u> interactivity, and <u>more</u> control. Enter JavaScript and Java, two programming languages, to provide the <u>more</u> that developers needed.

Web pages communicate ideas by bringing together different media. One type of media, interactive programs, did not exist on the Web until JavaScript and Java became available. People who write programs that *do* things on Web pages use these programming languages. They add functionality to Web pages, just as helpers and plug-ins do, but they provide much greater flexibility. JavaScript is usually integrated with the Web page and runs on the client side. Java is usually integrated on the server side.

The first two addresses will connect you to some really interesting examples of Java.

The Impressionist
http://reality.sgi.com/employees/paul_asd/impression/index.html
Crossword Puzzle
http://home.netscape.com/comprod/products/navigator/version_2.0/java_applets/Crossword

This last address will connect you to a rather large collection of both Java and JavaScript examples.

Gamelan
http://www.developer.com/directories/pages/dir.java.html

Depending on your system, these examples may take a while to load so be patient.

Customizing

You know now how to handle some very important aspects of the Internet. Perhaps at this point you want to fine-tune your set-up. Want to change your home page? Want to change the typeface your screen shows? Let's look at a few options.

Home Page

You might want to modify the location of your home page, which is the screen that appears every time you start up your browser. If you're working with a browser that hasn't been customized before, the company that made the browser probably chose the home page. If you're working on one of your school's computers, then the home page may already be set to the school's page. Find out if you are permitted to change the home page in your computer lab. If it's okay to do so, then decide what you want to set as your home page. By now you've probably found something on the Web that you would want to call home. When *your* home page is properly set, every time you start your browser or select home from the toolbar, you'll end up at this place, so choose wisely. (However, you can always change your home page again if you want to.)

In Netscape, click on the *Edit* menu and then *Preferences*. If you next highlight Navigator, you should get the page that appears in Figure 3.6. Type in the address of whatever you want for your home page in the *Location* box.

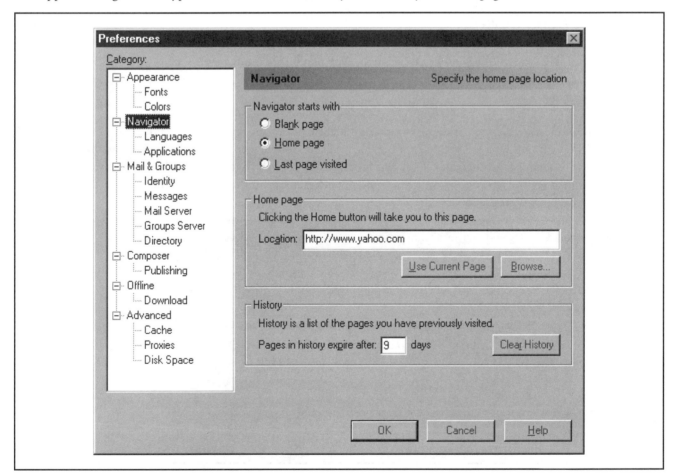

Figure 3.6. Navigator lets you set your home page to any screen you'd like. Just type in the appropriate address. This browser is set to call Yahoo! home.

Setting Options

On the Internet, as in the rest of life, *time is money*. Saving time is important if you have to use a modem and an Internet service provider (ISP) to cruise the Net. One way to speed up your Internet travels is to change the *Automatically Load Images* option. The images that appear on the Net's pages make it an attractive place to visit, but loading these images takes time. You might, then, want to turn this option off. Click on *Edit* on the toolbar and select *Preferences*. Now move to *Advanced* (see Figure 3.7). The checkmark in the box means that the images will load. If you click in the box to eliminate the checkmark, Net pages will appear on your screen without the time-consuming images. Try it to see how much more quickly pages load. If you want to restore the *Automatically Load Images* function, just click in the box one more time. The checkmark will reappear, signaling that your browser will again load the Net's images.

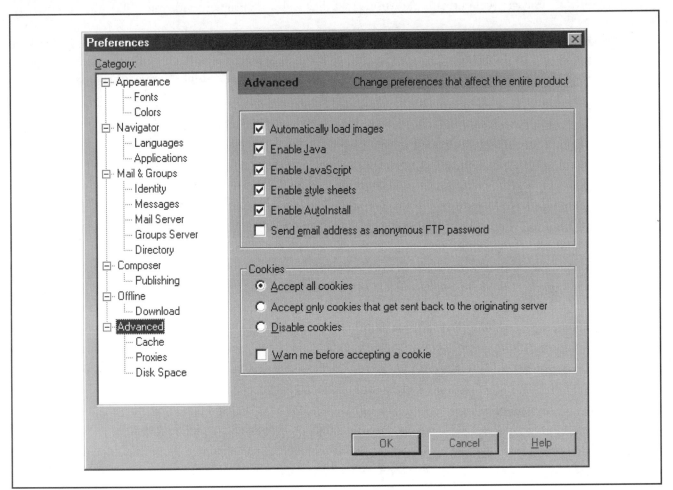

Figure 3.7. Netscape allows you to set many options, among them whether or not images automatically load onto your screen. A checkmark indicates that images will appear.

Other Options

Go to the top bar of Navigator and click on *View*. Note the various options that appear. For example, if you want to eliminate the personal toolbar, simply click on *Hide Personal Toolbar*. To restore it, pull down the *View* menu again and click on *Show Personal Toolbar*.

Clicking on the word *Edit* on the top of the toolbar lets you set still other options. After pulling down the *Edit* menu, click on *Preferences*. Note the range of options you can set, including font and colors.

Although we have not discussed all of the options, you have enough experience now to explore. Experiment with the settings on your own. However, you do need to be careful. Some options won't apply to your setup. With other options, you will need specific information to ensure that they will work properly with your ISP.

Whatever your question – about setting options or about some other aspect of Netscape — you'll be pleased to know that Netscape provides a wide range of help topics. Just click on the word *Help* on the top of the toolbar. From the submenu that appears, choose the top item, *Help Contents*. If you are using Microsoft's Internet Explorer or another browser, you will find that they have very similar features.

Chapter 4
Online Job Searches and Résumés

On the Internet, career development is just a mouse-click away. You may already be familiar with traditional job-search resources such as the *Occupational Outlook Handbook* (for identifying high-growth occupations), *What Color Is Your Parachute?* (for practical tips on how to get a job), and the help-wanted ads in your local newspaper. Now the Internet has many of the same resources online and ready for instant access—along with an ever-expanding variety of additional job-related Web sites.

Whether you're looking for a new job or want to explore an entirely new occupation, you can gather a great deal of information without leaving your keyboard. By launching your Web browser and moving onto the Internet, you will be able to search for career opportunities, find job openings in your chosen field, investigate potential employers, exchange ideas with other job-seekers, and enlarge your circle of contacts.

Remember that changes on the Internet occur almost daily, so you are bound to find something new or different every time you log on. From career counseling centers to job-search newsgroups, virtual job fairs to commercial résumé databanks, more and more Internet options are becoming available to help bring employers and potential employees together.

This constant change also means that your favorite Web site may have new features or even a new location next time you go online. As a result, don't be surprised to find a slightly different look or perhaps a new address for the sites mentioned in this chapter.

How to Research Careers and Employers

A good way to start your online job search is by researching various occupations and industries that sound appealing. This way, you can identify career paths that match your interests, see which have strong potential for future growth, and then focus your search accordingly.

To learn more about specific occupations, bookmark the latest edition of the *Occupational Outlook Handbook*, from the U.S. Department of Labor. This multi-faceted site describes a wide range of occupations, detailing each job's duties, training requirements, employment trends, and future prospects (http://stats.bls.gov/ocohome.htm). For the latest news about employment projections, earnings, and the effect of regional economic conditions, check the news releases posted online by the U.S. Bureau of Labor Statistics (http://stats.bls.gov/newsrels.htm).

Many state employment offices maintain Web sites bursting with comprehensive information about occupations, industries, wages, and many other topics. You can locate your state's job service site by launching Excite or another search tool and searching for "state employment service" or a similar phrase. Once you find your state's site, be sure to explore each hyperlink—you never know where these connections will lead you.

For example, the Career Resource Library on the New York State Department of Labor Web site (http://ny.jobsearch.org/library.htm) contains a wealth of hyperlinks to state and regional employment trends and projections; national, statewide, and local wage rates; industry descriptions; and hyperlinks to dozens of other sites with tips on vital subjects such as résumé preparation, training and education, job applications, and interviewing (see Figure 4.1). Even job-seekers outside New York will be interested in the general guidance available on this site.

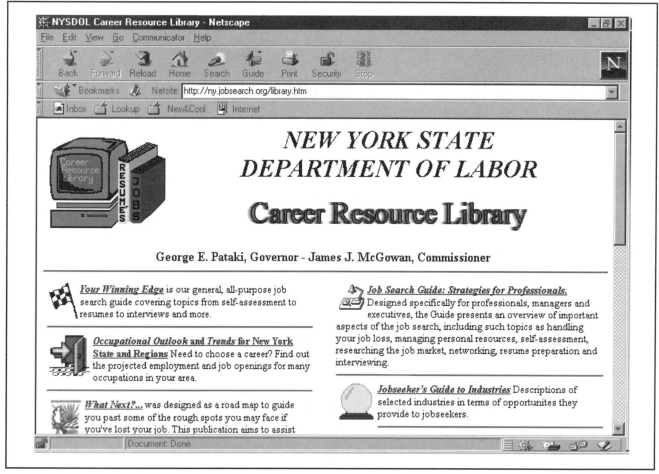

Figure 4.1. Check out the career research library at the Web site of the New York State Department of Labor.

Be sure to find out about your school's career services, which are often available online through the campus placement office. In addition, you may want to browse other university career counseling Web sites for more information about various occupations. Here are just two samples: The "Career Exploration Links" maintained by the University of California at Berkeley (http://www.uhs.berkeley.edu/CareerLibrary/links/occup.cfm) and the "Exploring Occupations" page from the University of Manitoba (http://www.umanitoba.ca/counselling/careers.html) both offer hyperlinks to pages describing dozens of occupations.

Some of the major online services and search tools maintain special areas for job-seekers. These areas generally feature career-planning advice, job postings, résumé preparation tips, and other useful information. You may also be able to join a job-search newsgroup, participate in an online chat about how to interview well, or read messages posted by others who are in the job market.

For instance, visit Yahoo! and go to its employment area, which is located under the business category (http://www.yahoo.com/Business/Employment/). On this page, you can scroll through a variety of help-wanted classified ads, post your résumé for employers to consider, or drop into an interesting job-related online chat. Events and job openings change daily, so check back often.

Once you have narrowed your search to a particular occupation or industry, you can begin to study potential employers. If you know the names of companies in your targeted field, you can use an Internet search tool to locate their Web sites. Of course, these company sites are designed for promotion, so don't expect them to be objective sources of information. Still, you can get a good idea of what the company does, where it operates, and how it views its business situation.

Another way to locate company Web sites is through hyperlinks on the larger career Web sites such as Espan (http://www.espan.com) and Career Mosaic (http://www.careermosaic.com). For example, you can get more information about companies that recruit from the Espan site by clicking on each employer's hyperlink. In some cases, the hyperlink leads to the company's regular Web site. In other cases, the hyperlink leads to a special recruitment page. If you click on the name of Allstate on Espan's employer page, you will be connected to the insurance company's career site, which covers career opportunities, internships, benefits, and general information.

How to Find Job Openings

More and more job openings are being posted on the Internet—and not just for high-tech occupations. As you investigate any potential employer's Web site, look carefully for a hyperlink to that company's listing of job vacancies. These hyperlinks may be labeled "career opportunities," "recruitment," or some similar title.

As you might expect, computer makers such as Dell (http://www.dell.com) and Internet-based businesses such as Amazon.com (http://www.amazon.com) routinely post job openings on their Web sites and invite submission of electronic résumés. But you will also find a wide range of other firms recruiting applicants directly from their Web sites. The retail chain J.C. Penney (http://www.jcpenney.com/) and the global household products manufacturer Unilever (http://www.unilever.com) are just two of many employers that promote job openings on their Web pages.

Another way to find job openings on the Web is to visit virtual career fairs, where employers and job-seekers meet online. As in any career fair, you can find out more about participating employers, explore their immediate and anticipated job openings, submit your résumé for consideration, and (sometimes) have an initial cyberspace interview.

Look for career fairs listed on career sites such as Monster Board (http://www.monster.com), on search sites such as Yahoo (http://www.yahoo.com/Business_and_Economy/Employment/Jobs/Job_Fairs/), and on dedicated job-fair sites such as the Virtual Job Fair (http://www.vjf.com).

Help-wanted classified ads and job databanks are available on a variety of Web sites. Best Jobs USA (http://www.bestjobsusa.com), a Web site maintained by *Employment Review* magazine, invites job-seekers to search its listings of jobs by state, job category, company name, or special skill. You may also want to bookmark the career Web site maintained by the *Wall Street Journal* (http://careers.wsj.com/). Here, you can use the "Job Seek" function to search posted job openings by industry, type of job, company, and location. If you choose, you can add your name to an e-mailing list at this site so you will be alerted when new employers and new features become available.

Newspaper classified ads, a traditional source of leads for new jobs, are increasingly common on the Web. For example, if you live in the Boston area—or if you want to relocate there—you may want to search the *Boston Globe's* online employment classifieds (http://careers.boston.com/). You can use *Yahoo!* or another search tool to locate the Web sites of newspapers in specific cities. In addition, hyperlinks to leading newspapers are available at the Info Service Web site (http://info-s.com/paper6.html) and at Ecola, which serves as a gateway to dozens of U.S. publications (http://www.ecola.com/news/press/na/us/).

Some sites compile listings of help-wanted ads drawn from dozens of newspapers. One good example is the CareerPath Web site (http://www.careerpath.com). This site also lists job openings that have been posted on company Web sites, a time-saving feature that allows you to search job listings by state, name of employer, industry, and/or type of job.

If you want to post your résumé and invite prospective employers to find you, take time to investigate the growing number of résumé databanks available on the Internet. You can find listings of the largest databanks—as well as those that specialize in particular occupations—by checking career Web sites such as Job Hunt (http://www.jobhunt.org/resume.shtml) and the Job Resource (http://solimar1.stanford.edu/), which was started by students from Stanford University.

Employers that recruit online generally prefer to receive electronic résumés rather than the usual printed résumés. The next section shows how you can prepare your résumé for electronic submission to employers and databanks.

How to Create an Electronic Résumé

Just as you are using your PC to search for employers and jobs via the Internet, a growing number of employers are using computers to store and search through all the résumés they receive from applicants. Instead of spending hours sifting through a mountain of cover letters and printed résumés, a manager can now enter a few key words or phrases to describe the required skills and qualifications for a particular job opening. In short order, the computer will bring up a listing of all the electronic résumés in the database that fit those exact specifications. Only applicants whose résumés are in the computer system will be considered for such job opportunities—which is why *you* need an electronic résumé.

If you have already created a résumé using a word-processing program, a few simple changes will get it into shape for submission to company computer systems and commercial résumé databanks. Start by opening the file containing your résumé, then saving it as a plain ASCII text file; change the name, if you want, to distinguish this text-only version from the fully-formatted version.

Because text-only files cannot accommodate fancy fonts, be sure your résumé appears in one simple font and one font size. Remove any formatting such as boldface, underlining, and italics. Also remove justification, tables, rules, and columns. If you have tabs in your document, remove them and use the space bar to align your text. Then change every bullet to an asterisk or a lower-case letter *o*, as shown in Figure 4.2.

Roberto Cortez

5687 Crosswoods Drive
Falls Church, Virginia 22046

Home: (703) 987-0086   Office: (703) 549-6624

OBJECTIVE

Accounting management position requiring a knowledge of international finance

EXPERIENCE

March 1993 to present	Staff Accountant/Financial Analyst, Inter-American Imports(Alexandria, VA)

- Prepare accounting reports for wholesale giftware importer with annual sales of $15 million
- Audit financial transactions with suppliers in 12 Latin American countries
- Created a computerized model to adjust accounts for fluctuations in currency exchange rates
- Negotiated joint-venture agreements with major suppliers in Mexico and Columbia

October 1989 to March 1993	Staff Accountant, Monsanto Agricultural Chemicals (Mexico City, Mexico)

- Handled budgeting, billing, and credit-processing functions for the Mexico City branch
- Audited travel/entertainment expenses for Monsanto's 30-member Latin American sales force
- Assisted in launching an online computer system (IBM)

EDUCATION

1989 to 1993	MBA with emphasis on international business George Mason University (Fairfax, Virginia)
1985 to 1989	BBA, Accounting Universidad Naçional Autónoma de Mexico (Mexico City, Mexico)

INTERCULTURAL QUALIFICATIONS

- Born and raised in Mexico City; became U.S. citizen in 1991
- Fluent in Spanish and German
- Traveled extensively in Latin America

References available on request

Résumé Submitted in Confidence

Figure 4.2. This résumé may serve as a good model for how to prepare your own electronic résumé as you use the Web to learn more about job opportunities.

The first line of your résumé should contain only your full name. Type your street address, phone and fax numbers, and e-mail address on separate lines below your name. Next, count the number of characters in each line—and create a new line whenever the number of characters (including spaces) exceeds 65. This ensures that your electronic résumé will look neat when a potential employer brings it up on the screen.

Knowing that employers search their résumé databases according to key words, you should include a *key word* section near the top of your résumé. To do this, compile a list of nouns that describe your job-related skills and abilities. Some of these nouns may already be contained in your résumé, but you will also want to highlight them by positioning them in the key word section.

For example, depending on your work experience, you will want to include appropriate job titles (such as "supervisor" or "team leader") in the key word section. Similarly, if you have experience with a specialized area such as exchange rates, list the phrase "exchange rates" in your key word section. Be sure to highlight your full range of accomplishments, including such skills as fluency in other languages and any official certification courses you have completed.

Once you have completed work on your résumé, be sure to save it again as an ASCII plain text file. If you prepare separate electronic résumés for different employers or job openings, save those in separate ASCII files so you can easily access them when needed. To be sure that your electronic résumé looks good, copy and paste it into an e-mail message to yourself or to a friend. Once the e-mail message has been received, you will be able to spot and correct any formatting errors.

Remember that all the usual rules about writing a good résumé also apply to your electronic résumé: Showcase your strongest qualifications; summarize your work experience with an emphasis on results and achievements; mention relevant activities and talents; and use correct spelling and grammar. Above all, be honest. If you misrepresent your background, you may find yourself out of a job when your new employer finds out.

To get an idea of what other traditional and electronic résumés look like, you may want to browse the career sites, which often feature sample résumés. In addition, you can launch your news reader and access the newsgroup **misc.jobs.resumes**, where you will find many résumés posted.

Also seek out Web sites that offer general advice about résumés, both traditional and electronic. Among the many academic sites you can browse are the site sponsored by Purdue University (**http://owl.english.purdue.edu/Files/35 .html**) and the site sponsored by the College of William & Mary (**http://www.wm.edu/csrv/career/stualum/resmdir/ contents.html**)

Information about electronic résumés is also available at the America's Job Bank Web site, which is operated by the Public Employment Service (**http://www.ajb.dni.us/html/eresume.html#prep**) and at the Online Career Center, where the author of Electronic Résumé Revolution has posted her top tips (**http://www.occ.com/occ/jlk/ howtoeresume.html**). Both sites feature job openings and hyperlinks to a variety of career development resources. Resumix®, which provides human resource software solutions for large corporations, also offers instructions and helpful tips on how to prepare the most effective electronic résumés. The Resumix Web site (**http://www.resumix. com/resume/resumeindex.html**) can guide you step-by-step through the process of drafting an electronic résumé (see Figure 4.3).

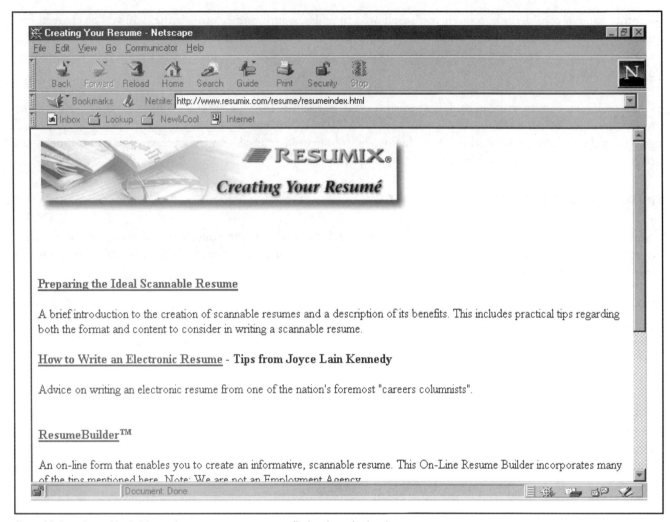

Figure 4.3. Resumix provides insights on how you can create a most effective electronic résumé.

Once you have polished your electronic résumé, should you submit it to one or more résumé databanks? Uploading your résumé to be included in a larger databank of résumés is not the same as sending your résumé to a single employer's résumé database. The employer is going to keep your résumé in its proprietary computer system, to be accessed only by company personnel who are searching for applicants to fill job openings. Commercial résumé databanks, however, are open to many employers, which raises several issues for you to consider.

Be aware that submitting your résumé to a commercial databank makes your private information available to many people. If you have security concerns about publicizing your home address and phone number, you may want to omit these details—or follow the advice of one expert, who recommends arranging for a post office box and answering service with a separate phone number to handle inquiries during the job-search period.

In addition, before you post your electronic résumé on any databank, find out who is allowed to access the résumés. Also ask whether you will be notified when an employer requests your résumé—and whether you can limit access to prevent specific organizations (such as your current employer) from requesting your résumé.

Another issue to consider is how often you are allowed to update your résumé, and whether you will be charged for doing so. At some point, you may need to correct a spelling error or add a new skill you recently acquired. Find out whether updates are permitted and, if you are expected to pay for updates, continue looking until you find a suitable databank that permits free updates.

Finally, ask each commercial databank how often it removes résumés from its system. Employers want to see only up-to-date résumés, which is why some databanks get rid of older résumés after a certain number of months. So investigate the policy of any commercial databank before you submit your résumé—and, if necessary, plan to submit updated résumés at regular intervals throughout your job search.

How to Contact Employers Online

Now that your electronic résumé is ready, you can move full speed ahead with your job search, checking both traditional and Internet sources for employment openings. When you find an intriguing job opening, carefully follow the employer's instructions for applying electronically.

Some employers that post job openings on the Internet require applicants to fill out an online form, typing in name, address, and other details. In many cases, you will notice a large box near the bottom of the online form. This is where you are expected to paste the plain text version of your résumé (after copying it from the ASCII file). The employer may also ask you to insert a reference code or word somewhere on the form, to identify the opening for which you are applying.

At times, you will find that a job opening posted on the employer's Web site is accompanied by hyperlink that leads to a pre-addressed e-mail message form. Again, follow the employer's instructions for completing the message. If you are instructed to type in a job title or reference number, place these according to the employer's instructions, then follow the employer's exact directions for submitting your résumé.

If you are responding to a help-wanted ad in a newspaper or some other medium, you can apply by e-mail if the employer includes an e-mail address. Launch your Web browser or Internet communication program, bring up a blank message screen, and type the employer's e-mail address in the *To* field. If the ad includes a job title or reference number, always include that information in the *Subject* field.

Next, type a very brief cover letter in the *Message* field, explaining that you are applying for the advertised position and stating your strongest qualifications (see Figure 4.4). You can't actually sign your letter, but you can type a polite complimentary closing, press the *Enter* key twice, and type your full name. Finally, copy and paste your electronic résumé below the cover letter in the *Message* field. Take a minute to reread the message—checking spelling and spacing—before you actually press the *Send* button.

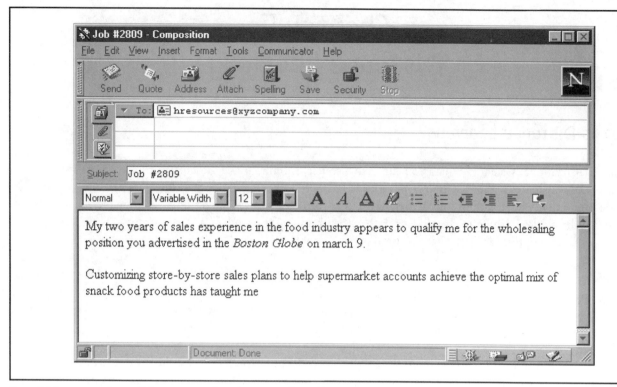

Figure 4.4. You can use the e-mail feature on your browser to communicate with potential employers.

For more information about writing an effective cover letter, point your browser to Brandeis University's Hiatt Career Development Center Web site (http://www.brandeis.edu/hiatt/web_data/hiatt_cover_letter.html) or the State University of New York at Buffalo's Career Planning & Placement Web site (http://www.ub-careers.buffalo.edu/career/resume/coverlet.html).

Never send your electronic résumé as an attachment to an e-mail message unless an employer specifically requests this transmission method. Given the diversity of word-processing programs in use in the business world, your résumé may not be compatible with the employer's software—which means that your résumé will not become part of that company's database.

Companies that encourage e-mail submission of résumés are generally receptive to e-mail messages as follow-ups to job-search activities such as interviews. Rather than print and mail a thank-you letter after an interview, for example, you can send your company contact an e-mail message with the same information. When composing a thank-you message, refer to the interview in your *Subject* line by typing "Thank you for the October 26 interview" or a similar brief phrase in the subject line.

After you have typed the body of your message, include a business-like complimentary closing, press the *Enter* key twice, and type your full name. Then type your address, your phone and fax numbers, and your e-mail address on separate lines directly below your name. After all, you want to make it as easy and convenient as possible for potential employers to contact you.

Good luck!

Chapter 5
Distance Learning

What is Distance Learning?

Imagine an educational system in which you can take a course, submit an assignment, even interact with your instructor and classmates without stepping into a real classroom—that's distance learning. As the name implies, students are physically separated from instructors (and often from each other) in a distance learning arrangement. The purpose is to bring the learning to the student, rather than bringing the student to the learning—providing more flexibility and more options for personal and professional growth.

As a student, you can participate in distance learning in a variety of ways. In some programs, you receive instruction and assignments via the Internet, using e-mail, audio streaming, video clips, group chats, or other techniques; in other programs, you watch your instructor on videotape, videoconference, or television. Your alternatives for distance learning will depend on the provider of the course you select.

In early distance learning programs, students watched televised lectures (on regularly-scheduled programs with titles such as *Sunrise Semester*) and then mailed completed assignments to the college for grading and credit. Today, some form of distance learning is available at more than half of all four-year colleges and universities in the United States—and many offer degree programs entirely by Internet.

For example, the Colorado Electronic Community College (http://www.ccconline.org) offers an Internet-only associate degree program. Similarly, the University of Phoenix (http://www.uophx.edu/online/) offers Internet-only undergraduate and graduate degrees. These types of programs allow students to use the Internet for almost everything, from ordering textbooks and filling out financial aid forms to downloading course materials and taking quizzes.

Distance learning is also becoming more popular at colleges and universities around the world, from Aston University in the United Kingdom (http://www.les.aston.ac.uk/home.html) to Macquarie University in Australia (http://www.elm.mq.edu.au).

Colleges are not the only sources of distance learning programs. Employers have begun to embrace distance learning in its many forms. As one example, the Tennessee Valley Authority offers career enrichment courses by videotape and by self-paced computer training, in addition to its traditional classroom courses. As another example, employees of GTE Corporation can attend educational videoconferences on personal finance as well as participate in job-related courses.

Professional organizations such as the Illinois Association of Realtors are also using distance learning on the Internet to provide continuing education training to their members. And distance learning is now being developed by some companies as a profit-making venture. ZDNet University (http://www.zdu.com) is a good example. An offshoot of Ziff-Davis, which publishes magazines on information technology, ZDNet University offers courses on Internet technology and its business applications.

Distance is no object when you are able to access learning materials via the Internet. Whether a course originates in another city, state, or country, all students receive the same lectures, assignments, and attention. As a result, a student in the United States can sign up for an education class at the University of Birmingham in England (http://sun4.bham.ac.uk), while a student in California can log onto a course in speech writing offered by Syracuse University Continuing Education Online in New York state (http://www.suce.syr.edu/online/).

Wherever you are, whatever you want to learn, you can probably find a distance learning course somewhere in the world to meet your needs.

Advantages and Disadvantages

Distance learning on the Internet has many advantages. At the top of the list is the broad array of choices. You can earn a degree, obtain continuing education credits, sharpen your work skills, prepare for a new job or career, stay abreast of fast-changing technology, even master a new subject for personal enrichment—all without leaving your keyboard.

Easy access is another major advantage. As long as you have the right computer hardware and software as well as a connection to the Internet, you can be a distance learning student. Just log onto the course's Web site to download the latest lecture, or enter the designated chat room for a cyberspace exchange of ideas. If you have a laptop computer with modem, you can easily send in your course assignments from home, office, or almost anywhere.

Most of the time, distance learning on the Internet allows you to work at your own pace, an important advantage for people who are juggling school and work responsibilities and those whose schedules can change from day to day. Rather than having to be in the classroom at a particular time, distance learning students can usually access a Web site at any hour to read new assignments or e-mail the instructor with questions.

Distance learning on the Internet can save you money, even though some undergraduate and graduate courses are more costly than traditional classroom courses. For example, tuition for one credit hour at the Colorado Electronic Community College is more than twice the price of one credit hour of on-campus study. Still, by using the Internet for distance learning, you completely avoid charges for room and board (or the cost of traveling to class), which can represent a significant savings.

Of course, distance learning on the Internet has disadvantages, as well. One key disadvantage is the lack of live interaction with the instructor and with classmates. If you thrive on classroom debate or prefer to have your questions answered immediately, you may not like having to type your comments or wait for an e-mailed response.

Some programs have addressed this issue by arranging for periodic desktop videoconferencing. Students and instructors place small videocameras on their computer monitors and speak into microphones to participate in group discussions during a desktop videoconference session. Students can see the instructor, the instructor can see the students, and everybody can hear every comment.

Another disadvantage is the need for access to an appropriately configured personal computer and an Internet connection in order to take an online course. In response, some schools are inviting their distance learning students to use the computer facilities on campus or at regional satellite centers.

Overall, distance learning is best suited to students who are motivated to assume responsibility for their own learning. You must be willing to log onto the course Web site at regular intervals; download and review instructional materials; and post your questions or ask for additional help.

Remember, some courses require students to visit chat rooms for group discussions; some mandate frequent or lengthy homework projects; others expect students to read and comment on classmates' reports and projects. You have to be ready to invest sufficient time and effort to meet all these course requirements. You must also have the flexibility to deal with the occasional technical glitches that can crop up. Only you can decide whether distance learning is right for <u>you</u>.

How to Find Information About Distance Learning

In an earlier chapter, you learned how to search for information using directories and search engines. Now you can apply your search skills to scour the World Wide Web for information about distance learning classes and resources.

A Yahoo! Search

First, try using Yahoo! to conduct this search. Start by connecting to the Internet and launching your Web browser. In the location box (designated as "Go to" in Netscape Navigator), type in the address for Yahoo! (http://www. yahoo.com) and press the enter key on your keyboard.

Once the Yahoo! home page appears (Figure 5.1), you will see a search box near the top of the screen. Type in the words "distance learning" in quotation marks and click on the search button to begin your search for Web documents containing that exact phrase.

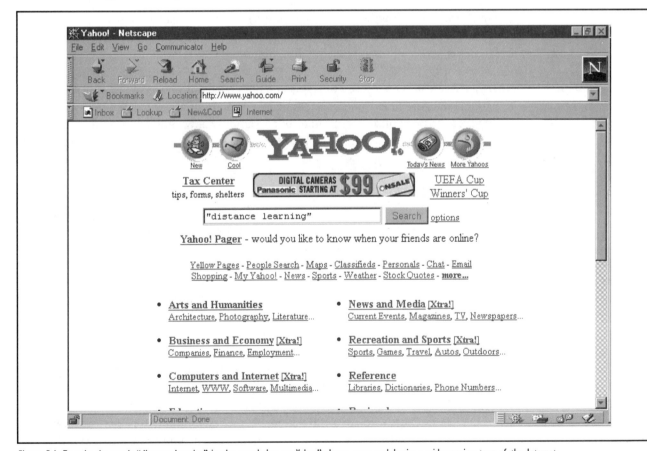

Figure 5.1. Type in the words "distance learning" in the search box on Yahoo!'s home page and begin a wide-ranging tour of the Internet.

Within a few seconds, you will be presented with a listing of category matches and Web sites, arranged alphabetically. Depending on your particular interest, you can click on the hyperlinks that lead to more information about specific types of courses or geographic locations of institutions and sponsors offering distance learning opportunities. Bear in mind that Web sites and hyperlinks are subject to change, so your search results are likely to differ from the examples and illustrations in this guide.

The broadest category on this initial list is titled "Education: Distance Learning" (see Figure 5.2). Click on that hyperlink to see a more detailed listing of distance learning resources.

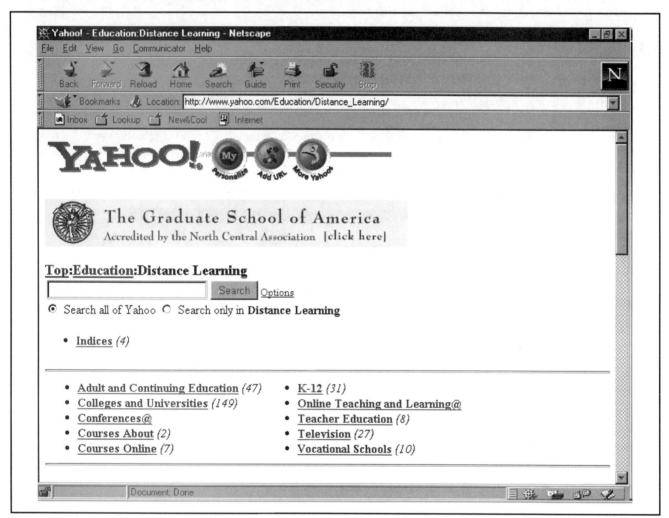

Figure 5.2. From this Yahoo! Page you can click on the hyperlinks that will carry you to categories of courses, colleges, and other education opportunities.

This page in the Yahoo! directory serves as a general guide to all types of distance learning courses. Notice that you can click on hyperlinks for categories of courses, including adult and continuing education; colleges and universities; and other types of courses. The number in parentheses next to the category name indicates how many hyperlinks are available for that subject.

Below the categories are individual hyperlinks to additional resources, including sites that list distance learning opportunities and sites that offer information about distance learning theory and techniques. You can click on any hyperlink, explore the contents, and then click the *Back* button on the browser toolbar to jump back to the Yahoo! search results and explore more hyperlinks. Also, use the Yahoo! search facility to quickly find specific words or phrases (such as "business") embedded in the categories and hyperlinks on a particular page—or throughout the entire Yahoo! site.

What if you want to find out more about colleges and universities offering distance learning courses? Simply click on that hyperlink in the Yahoo! search results, and you will be presented with several subcategories, including community colleges and graduate programs, plus an alphabetical listing of sources for classes and more information. Now you can click on any hyperlink to go immediately to that site.

A Metacrawler Search

When you search for the same phrase in another search tool, your results will be somewhat different. To see how this works, try using Metacrawler to search for distance learning courses. Metacrawler conducts a simultaneous search on six directories and search engines: Webcrawler, Excite, Yahoo!, Infoseek, Lycos, and AltaVista.

You can reach the Metacrawler Web site through your Web browser by typing the address (**http://www.metacrawler. com**) in the location box. With Metacrawler's home page on your screen (see Figure 5.3), type the phrase "distance learning" in the search box, click the *as a phrase* option, select *the Web*, and click the *search* button.

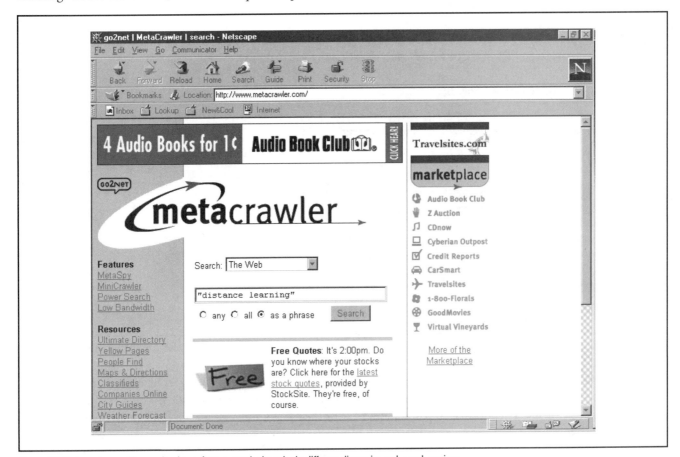

Figure 5.3. Metacrawler provides results drawn from a search through six different directories and search engines.

A few seconds will pass as Metacrawler compiles the answers it is receiving from each of the six search tools. Then you will see a detailed listing of the results, ranked according to the numeric score that indicates the relevancy of each site (see Figure 5.4). You can now read the description of each site before you click on the hyperlink. Metacrawler speeds you through the results by highlighting the search word or phrase in bold in the title or description of each site.

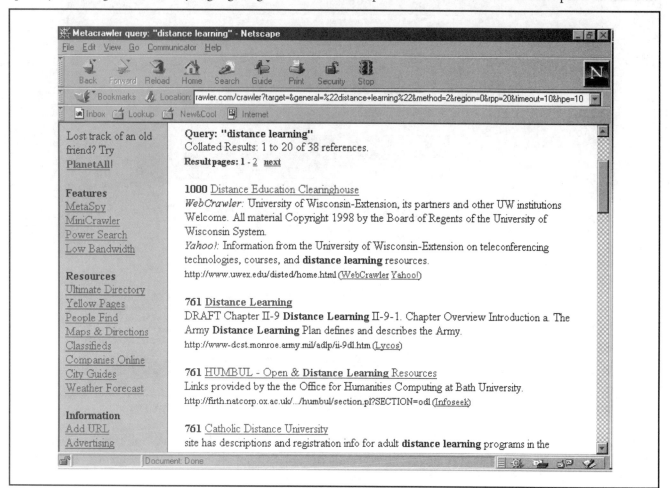

Figure 5.4. This screen shows you the first twenty of thirty-eight references Metacrawler found while searching "distance learning."

A Newsgroup Search

You can also use Webcrawler to locate newsgroups about distance learning. Simply type "distance learning" in the search box, select *newsgroups*, and then click the *search* button. The results will show descriptions of messages that have been posted to newsgroups (see Figure 5.5).

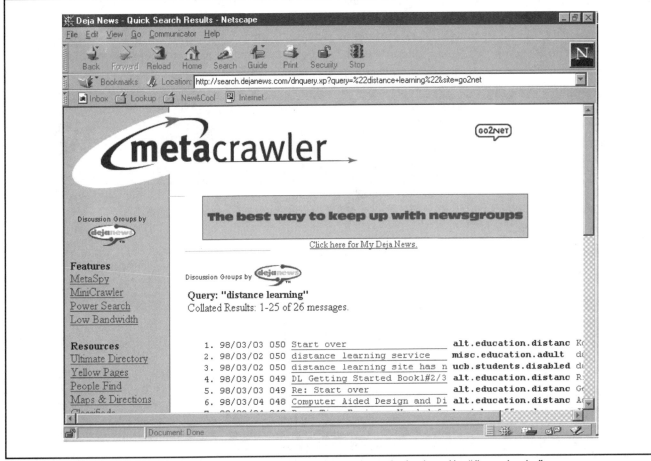

Figure 5.5. Metacrawler also searches for newsgroups. This screen shows some newsgroups Metacrawler found searching "distance learning."

To read an interesting message, just click on that hyperlink to bring up a screen showing the full text. You will also see the name and e-mail address of the author, in case you want to follow up by e-mailing a comment or question. If you find that a number of relevant messages have been posted to one or more newsgroups, you may want to subscribe so you can receive any subsequent postings and join the discussion by posting your own messages. However, be aware that many newsgroups contain commercial postings as well as a wide range of personal opinions, so use good judgment to analyze and evaluate what you read.

Although these examples have focused on searches for "distance learning," you should try searches using other words or phrases to locate additional resources. For example, a search for "distance education" on the Web or in newsgroups will result in a different listing of hyperlinks. Remember that Web sites and newsgroups are constantly changing, so your results will probably look different from the results shown here—and any searches you conduct in the future are likely to return different results from those you conduct today.

A Distance Learning Sampler

To supplement your search efforts, you may want to take a few minutes to browse the following Web sites, just a small sample of the many distance learning opportunities available on the Internet. Some of these sites contain hyperlinks to other programs or additional sources of information that can be useful as you expand your search.

General Information

- Is distance learning right for you? Take this short online self-test from Waukesha County Technical College, WI—and find out. http://www.waukesha.tec.wi.us/pro.htm

- Tips for success: how to get the most from any distance learning opportunity, from the College of DuPage, IL. http://www.dupage.edu/excel.html

- Find and evaluate college-level distance learning courses using the Distance Learning Resource Network's listing of printed and Internet resources. http://www.fwl.org/edtech/CollegeDistanceEd.html

- Browse categorized listings of hyperlinks for distance learning programs, technology providers, and sources of information about distance learning theory and technique. http://www.online.uillinois.edu/ramage/disted.html

Academic Credit

- The National Universities Degree Consortium Web site offers hyperlinks to 14 accredited universities that coop eratively offer distance learning courses for undergraduate and graduate degrees as well as certificate programs. Members include Kansas State University and Colorado State University. http://www.sc.edu/deis/NUDC

- The West Suburban Post-Secondary Chicago consortium of colleges and universities provides online access to distance learning courses through members such as College of DuPage, Illinois State University, and North Central College. http://www.dupage.edu/wspsc/index.html

- At the Electronic University Network Web site, students can browse the virtual campuses and courses of sev eral colleges that offer online courses. http://www.wcc-eun.com/wln/campus/eun/index.html

- CASO's Internet University site contains a comprehensive listing of distance learning courses and providers with brief descriptions plus hyperlinks to more detailed data. http://www.caso.com/iu/courses.html

- University of Minnesota offers undergraduate degrees using a variety of distance learning techniques, including Internet-based instruction. http://www.cee.umn.edu/dis/

- Ohio University Independent Study allows students to earn credit toward undergraduate degrees using various distance learning techniques, including e-mail. http://www.cats.ohiou.edu/~indstu/index.htm

- University of Phoenix offers numerous undergraduate and graduate courses (and continuing education courses); cyberstudents can earn a bachelor's or master's degree entirely through online study. http://www.uophx.edu/

Career Development

- Certificate programs in telecommunications are available through distance learning programs on the Internet from the University College of the University of Denver; students can also earn undergraduate and graduate degrees in a number of disciplines. http://www.du.edu/ucol/tele/teleidx.html

- The Continuing Professional Education program at University of Phoenix (see Figure 5.6) offers range of courses for enhancing professional proficiency. Try a free online orientation course to preview the learning method before registering. http://www.uophx.edu/cpeinet/

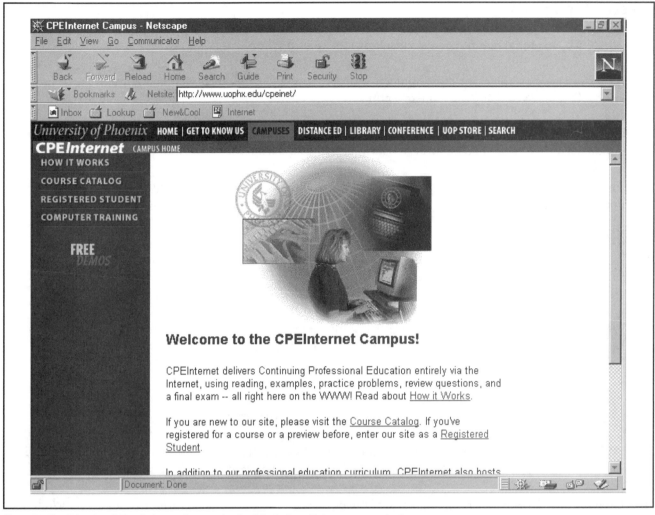

Figure 5.6. The University of Phoenix is one of many educational institutions offering courses on the Internet.

- The Indiana University School of Continuing Studies offers online certificate programs, credit and noncredit courses in labor studies, workforce development, and other management subjects. http://www.extend.indiana.edu/gs/cs.htm

- Professional certificates in accounting, business, and management are offered through the Internet by Champlain College Online in Vermont; associate and bachelor's degrees are also available. http://www.champlain.edu/OLDE/index.html

Personal Enrichment
- LearnItOnline from ZDNet (Ziff-Davis, publisher of tech magazines) offers online learning to help users get the most from programs such as Web browsers, word processing, and graphics software. http://www.learnitonline.com/

- Syracuse Continuing Education Online offers a variety of non-credit courses, including fiction writing, critical thinking, communication, psychology, and programming. http://www.suce.syr.edu/online/

- The WhaleNet educational Web site, from Wheelock College in Boston, has everything you wanted to know about whales (and marine life)—and more. http://whale.wheelock.edu/

- Take an online poetry course from Clark College, Washington, including cyberchat sessions and hyperlinks to online poets around the United States. http://clark.edu/instruct/human/english/poetry/poetry.htm

10 Questions to Ask Before You Register

No matter what goal you want to achieve by taking a distance learning course, you should ask pointed questions before making any commitments. A little advance checking will help you determine the potential benefits and value of each course under consideration. Just as important, these questions will help you recognize potential problems, eliminate inappropriate courses, and narrow your options to identify the courses most suited to your particular needs and situation.

1. Who is offering the course?

Find out about the institution, company, or organization offering the course. If the sponsor appears to be an educational institution, is it a real college or university (or a legitimate affiliate)? Names can be deceiving: what sounds like a prestigious university may actually be a front for a rip-off, so do some checking. Similarly, if a company or professional organization is sponsoring the course, you will want to investigate the sponsor's reputation and background before you sign a contract or send money.

The address of the Web site can often provide some clues (*.com* indicates a for-profit site, while *.edu* indicates an educational site). Also look for contact information such as the sponsor or institution's address, phone and fax numbers, affiliations, and other details.

2. Is the course part of an accredited program?

Accreditation is a critical issue for students seeking to earn a recognized degree. If a distance learning course is part of an unaccredited program, you may not be able to transfer the credits to an institution with an accredited program. If you are interested in pursing a degree entirely by distance learning and then continuing to study for even higher degrees, you should be sure that your diploma and coursework will be recognized by other institutions and by potential employers.

Legitimate educational institutions can provide solid information about their accreditation and refer you to the accrediting body for more details. Be especially careful about checking the accreditation of for-profit sponsors—and check on the accrediting body, as well. Accreditation is a complex topic, so you may want to talk with an administrator at a nearby college or university as an initial step.

3. What is the time commitment?

This is actually a two-part question. First, find out about the time requirements for an individual course. How often students must "meet" for cyberspace discussions (if ever)? How many meetings are required over the entire course? How much time is allowed for submitting assignments? How long you can expect the entire course to last? Must you log on a certain number of times or devote a given amount of time to coursework in order to obtain credit? For example, the Professional Real Estate Education Online program takes online attendance to ensure that students put in the required number of hours and complete the appropriate coursework to receive a certificate of completion.

Second, if you are planning to take distance learning courses to earn a degree, you will want to ask how many months or years students typically need to complete all their courses and qualify for graduation. In most cases, all courses are not offered all year-round, which can slow you down if you are trying to earn a degree more quickly. On the other hand, some institutions schedule courses more frequently, to accommodate students who are in a hurry. In addition, some institutions have regulations regarding the length of time a student can take to complete a degree, so check before you enroll.

4. What is the cost?

Ask about the tuition per course or per credit as well as any additional charges, such as registration or administration fees. Also ask about payment methods and schedules; nearly every school allows payment by major credit card, and some will accept payments in installments.

If textbooks or other learning materials must be purchased, take these into consideration when calculating the total cost of any distance learning course. Finally, consider the cost of dialing into the Internet to participate in the course.

5. What is the content?

Is the course merely an introduction to a topic—or is it an in-depth examination? Is the focus primarily on theory or will you also learn tips for practical application? Is the course covering the latest advances in the field? To answer these questions, you may have to go beyond the course description shown on the screen or in the catalog.

In some cases, you will have to contact the institution or sponsoring organization to get more details about the exact content of a particular course. Then ask yourself whether you are really interested in the course content—and whether the coverage will help you meet your goals.

6. What are the teacher's credentials?

Although some of what you learn in an online course will come from the text—and some from the comments and suggestions of other students—you will also want to look at your teacher's qualifications. How does the teacher's educational and/or work background fit with the course content? Has the teacher had much hands-on experience in applying what is being taught? How long has the teacher been teaching this or similar courses?

Many distance learning programs invite prospective students to read brief biographies of their faculty members. Before you sign up for a course, browse the Web site to read about the teachers so you can make an informed decision.

7. What are the entrance requirements or prerequisites?

As with traditional college or training programs, many distance learning programs impose entrance requirements or prerequisites. For example, some online master's or doctoral programs are open only to students with extensive work experience, just as some professional courses on the Internet are open only to those who have attained a particular standing or seniority in the industry.

A number of courses prevent students from enrolling in advanced courses unless they have taken lower-level courses as prerequisites. This is the case in many high-tech courses, where a basic knowledge of a particular programming language is generally required for admission. As a result, you should check on any requirements so you can plan to take courses in the appropriate order and at the appropriate point in your career.

8. How is the course conducted?

As discussed earlier, distance learning can take many forms. Before you sign up, you will want to take time to find out how your course will be conducted. Internet-based courses are often presented via a combination of e-mail, chat, electronic slide shows, and audio- or video-enhanced materials—in addition to a printed text. Some online courses may require a non-Internet component as well (such as teleconferencing).

A few schools allow students to try a sample class or course in advance; for example, Champlain College Online offers a sample course on Vermont history. Students simply sign up (http://www.champlain.edu/) and wait for e-mail instructions that explain how to log onto the system to access course materials.

As you investigate the way the course is conducted, also consider the communication between teachers and students. Are you expected to work individually or as part of a team of students to complete one or more class projects? How much e-mail interaction can you expect with the teacher? With other students? The answers to these questions will help you gauge whether a course fits your individual learning style and personal preferences.

9. What equipment is required?

At the very least, distance learning courses on the Internet require access to a properly-configured personal computer with modem, Web browsing software, and a dial-up connection to the Internet. Individual courses may require additional software, such as a word processing program for writing reports or technical software for completing assignments.

You can usually learn about equipment requirements in advance by reading the course description or checking the school's Web site for more information. If all else fails, send an e-mail to the institution or sponsor to inquire about the necessary equipment.

10. What assistance is available—and when?

In distance learning, students bear most of the responsibility for successful learning. However, there will be times when you decide to seek assistance. You may want guidance about courses; you may want help entering the Web site for a scheduled class "chat" session; or you may have some other problem or question. Some colleges and universities offer online assistance through self-guided tutorials or access to experts via e-mail. At Rogers University, for example, students can obtain academic counseling and career counseling by surfing the online counseling center on the school's Web site.

Be prepared: before you take any class, find out how and when you can obtain help. Although you may be eager to fix a problem at 2 a.m. so you can download an assignment right away, you may not be able to get help at that hour. So play it safe: ask for a name or department to contact and get a telephone number as well as an e-mail address in case you have an urgent request. You may even want to make a request to experience the help system first-hand before you register.

Learning in Cyberspace

How does a cyberstudent actually participate in a distance learning course on the Internet? The answer depends on the format of the course—and the student's individual learning style.

In this section, you will follow along as Vicky, an undergraduate cyberstudent enrolled in the University of Phoenix's online program, participates in the first week of a five-week Organizational Behavior course. Because this course is conducted entirely via online messages, the instructor's role is particularly critical.

The Instructor's Role

Chad Lewis, the instructor for this Organizational Behavior course, has been teaching online since the early days of Internet-based education. Following the University of Phoenix model, Chad carefully plans his courses to provide a distinct structure to the learning experience.

Online courses at University of Phoenix start on Thursdays, with each course divided into five weeklong "workshops" covering related topics. By the time his cyberstudents dial into the school's computer system on the first Thursday of the course, Chad has already posted his initial lecture notes and assignments. He will continue to post new lecture notes and assignments every Thursday until the final week of the course.

Throughout the five weeks, Chad goes online several times each day to read student messages, respond to their comments, and help those who have questions about the coursework or the mechanics. His written syllabus lets students know exactly when their assignments are due; he also requires class "participation"—students must read their classmates' answers and reports, then post responses. By sticking to an established timetable and maintaining an online active presence, Chad adds structure to the learning process—the online equivalent of attendance in a regularly-scheduled class in a physical school facility.

In addition, Chad carries on a private e-mail correspondence with each student. (Students can also call or fax instructors with any questions or concerns.) By noon on Saturdays, Chad makes it a point to have all homework graded and returned to his students' private mailboxes. This feedback allows students to track their progress. "In an online environment, instructors can never give students too much feedback," he says. "Students need to know how they are doing and what is expected of them."

Getting Ready for Class

Before Vicky can attend online classes at the University of Phoenix, she must apply for admission; register for each course; receive confirmation of acceptance into the class; install special software for class communication; and order the course materials (in this case, a textbook, a book of supplementary readings, and a course curriculum). Students are expected to log onto the class meeting at least five out of seven days so they can read messages and post responses. Because the coursework is so intense, students are allowed to take only one five-week class at a time.

When Vicky launches the school's software and logs onto the system Thursday morning, she finds two messages from Chad, her instructor. One contains his biography, with the request that students upload their own biographies to the class meeting as soon as possible.

The second message presents the course syllabus, with the content and assignments for each of the five week-long workshops. From that message, Vicky learns that each week-long workshop will follow a particular schedule:

- Thursday: The instructor posts a new lecturette in the "class meeting" section of the online system.
- Saturday: After reading the corresponding text materials, students upload answers to questions posed in the lecturette.
- Sunday: Students prepare either a case analysis or a short report and upload it to the "cases and reports" section of the online system.
- Wednesday: Students write and submit a brief summary of the most meaningful learning experiences gained from that week's workshop, including an analysis of how they can apply the knowledge in their work life.

After the first week, Vicky will be sure to check her private e-mailbox every Saturday for graded homework returned (with comments) by the instructor. Once she downloads and prints the syllabus and the first week's lecturette, she is ready to participate in the first workshop.

Class Is In Session

With syllabus in hand, Vicky is ready for the first week of the course.

Thursday

When Vicky comes home from work on Thursday, she writes a one-page biography, adds a sentence about the prospects for her local baseball team, and logs on to upload this message to the class meeting. Already, five of the 12 students have posted their biographies. Todd is an engineer working in Cleveland; Amelia is a nurse who has just moved to San Diego; Curtis is interviewing for a new manufacturing job in Houston; Roberto is a systems analyst in Nashville; and Cindy is an assistant manager in a New Haven store.

Vicky notices that Roberto has also posted a message for Curtis, asking whether any students from their previous online class will be in the Organizational Behavior class. To break the ice, Vicky posts a message for Todd, introducing herself and asking whether he knows her cousin, who works in Cleveland. Then she logs off, reads the lecturette, and starts reading the first of the two chapters required for that week's workshop, which focuses on the nature and functions of management.

Late Thursday evening, Vicky logs on again and downloads the biographies of four more students. She also finds a message from Todd, who doesn't know her cousin but does share her interest in baseball. Vicky posts a brief message for Chad, the instructor, to ask about the textbooks he has written. Then she logs off, ending her first day in that week's workshop.

Friday

At dinnertime on Friday, Vicky goes online to download the biographies of the last two students. Three other students have posted messages commenting on Vicky's biography and asking a question or two about her background. Chad has posted a response to Vicky's question (as well as responses to two other students' comments or questions).

Later that evening, Vicky finishes reading the second chapter in the textbook and the two supplemental readings. Then she logs on to the class meeting and reads the messages from the students who have posted their answers to the instructor's questions.

Saturday

On Saturday morning, Vicky rereads the lecturette questions. Then she drafts her answers, logs onto the system, and uploads her work. Next, she reads through all the other students' answers—making notes as she reads—then types her response to each. She questions one student's defense of scientific management, but agrees with another that total quality management is a key competitive tool, based on her company's experience in the global marketplace.

Later that day, Vicky writes a first draft of her case analysis, citing sources in the text and the supplemental readings. If she wants to look for extra sources to supplement the text, she can tap into the search facilities of the University of Phoenix's Web-based library resource.

Sunday

By mid-day Sunday, Vicky is back at her computer, putting the finishing touches on her case analysis. She logs onto the system, uploads this assignment, and then reads all the new messages. This is the fourth day of the workshop, and she has read through nearly 100 messages posted in the class meeting.

Reading and responding to her classmates' messages takes time, but the process gives Vicky a more in-depth understanding of the concepts and their application to real-world situations. In fact, as she reads the comments posted by other students, Vicky begins to rethink her own answers.

Tuesday

Although she is too busy on Monday to log on to the class meeting, Vicky goes online early Tuesday morning to read more messages and to respond to her classmates' comments about her case analysis. Some agree with her ideas, citing their own reading and on-the-job experiences, while some argue for a slightly different approach. Chad has responded to some of the student comments, as well. Rather than immediately respond, Vicky prints the messages and logs off to read them more carefully. Then, before dinner, she goes online again to post her responses and read the next batch of messages posted by her classmates.

Wednesday

On Wednesday morning, Vicky checks the class meeting for any last-minute postings. Then she logs off and makes notes for her summary of the most meaningful learning experiences gained from the first weekly workshop. At the top of her list is her new awareness of the diversity of functions that any manager in any organization must perform. Next, she writes about the lively debate over scientific management—and her belief that creative, empowered employees are the essential ingredient in peak organizational performance. She ends her summary with a commitment to developing her own conceptual skills, since her attention to detail sometimes obscures the big picture.

Logging on before dinner to upload her summary, Vicky takes a few minutes to read what other students have posted. After typing a few messages in response, she logs off for the day. The second weeklong workshop begins the next day, and Vicky wants to read ahead in preparation for the lecturette that will be posted in the class meeting on Thursday. It has been an intense week, but Vicky has enjoyed all the interaction with her classmates and she is looking forward to her instructor's comments on the homework assignment, which will be returned to her private e-mailbox on Saturday.

Class Is Over

During the fifth week of this Organizational Behavior course, Vicky downloads the final exam that Chad has posted in the class meeting. At this point, she has completed all the assignments and read through every online message posted by the instructor and the students. After she uploads the integrative report that serves as her final exam, she will wait a few days to find her final grades in her private e-mailbox—then the course will be over.

In addition to absorbing the basic concepts and thinking about their application to real work situations, Vicky has benefited from the insights offered by her diverse group of classmates. Although she has never actually seen Chad or any of her classmates, she feels as though she knows them through their online messages. Just as important, she was able to take the entire course without disrupting her ordinary work schedule, one of the key benefits of distance learning on the Internet.

Chapter 6
Using the Internet in Your Management Course

In previous chapters, you learned how to navigate the Internet and how to search for online information. Now you're ready to apply this knowledge to what you're learning in your management class and to on-the-job challenges.

This chapter presents brief descriptions and Internet addresses of nearly 100 World Wide Web sites that touch on management issues. Sites are listed alphabetically under each heading. Remember to bookmark the sites that are likely to be useful to you in the future.

The first section covers Web sites that help managers stay up-to-date on national and international news as well as on management concerns, business trends, and financial market results. The second section describes Web sites devoted to seven specific topics: general management; organizational behavior; human resource management; strategic management; small business and entrepreneurship; international business and management; and ethics. The third section describes Web sites that offer advice and guidance about how to manage your own management career.

Once you've become familiar with some of these Internet resources, you can gain experience in using the Internet by working through the sample class assignment that appears at the end of this chapter.

Note: Because the Internet is a dynamic medium, Web sites sometimes change, move, or disappear. Even though this guide was accurate when written, you may find that some of the sites look somewhat different or have moved to new locations.

Sources of Management Information

One of the many benefits of using the Internet is the ability to quickly locate updated information. Earlier in this guide, you learned how to use directories and search tools to hunt for online data. In this section, you will find descriptions of Web sites that can lead you to specific sources of management information.

Management Directories

Internet directories are good sources for broad coverage of management and business information. These directories tend to be encyclopedic, but most include a search engine to help narrow the focus of your search. The following is a representative sample of such directory sites.

Hotbot (http://www.hotbot.com)
The "Business & Finance" link brings you to an extensive listing of business-oriented categories such as professions, business to business, data and statistics, and regulation and government. The "Jobs, Careers & Work" link leads to "Workplace Issues" which links you to data about labor relations, privacy, and other concerns.

Infoseek (http://www.infoseek.com)
The "Business" channel includes briefings on news in 20 industries, descriptions of hundreds of companies, access to a business chat room, and summaries of the latest business news. This site is also available in Japanese, Spanish, and other languages.

Lycos (http://www.lycos.com)
You can find all kinds of business news, industry data, small business tips, and links to featured sites offering management and business advice about global business, taxes, and other important issues.

WebCrawler (http://www.webcrawler.com)
In the "Business & Investing" section, which is maintained by Quicken, you can see the latest financial market results, access small business information, and read about selected issues such as taxes, retirement plans, and insurance.

Yahoo! (http://www.yahoo.com)
The "Business and Economy" area on this popular Web site offers many categorized links to information about companies, economic indicators, ethics, marketing, small business, and much more, including a listing of business-related newsgroups.

In addition, a number of colleges, universities, and professional organizations offer Internet directories of useful management resources. The sites listed below are only a sample. Be sure to find out about resources that are available on your school's Internet site.

Academy of Management (http://www.aom.pace.edu)
This professional association for management research and education posts information about relevant journal articles, management conferences, special interest groups, and links to affiliated organizations (see Figure 6.1).

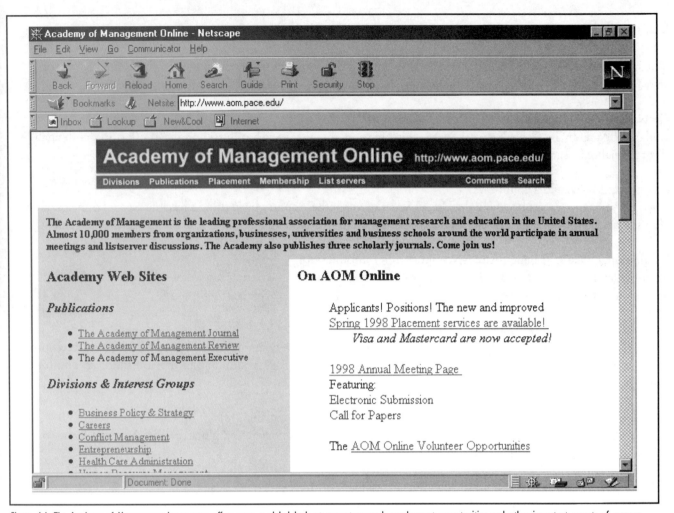

Figure 6.1. The Academy of Management home page offers users a global look at current research, employment opportunities, and other important aspects of management.

International Association for Management Education (http://www.aacsb.edu)
Check this site for information about management education conferences and publications about trends and issues in management education. In addition, the association has posted a list of links to related sites of interest.

Nijenrode University Library, the Netherlands (http://www.nijenrode.nl/nbr/)
A global compendium of online business resources arranged by category, with links to studies of specific regions of the world as well as to sources of information on economic issues, general management topics, and industry and marketing.

Prentice Hall Learning on the Internet Partnership (http://www.phlip.marist.edu)
Through a Web site at Marist College, Prentice Hall makes available textbook-related links, exercises, study assistance, and other information, organized according to business disciplines, including: management and organizational behavior, business communication, business law, strategy, and economics.

Current Regional, National, and International News

Managers who need to stay abreast of late-breaking news—in specific cities or states, around the United States, or anywhere in the world—can check the following sites, which cover a full range of newsworthy subjects.

CNN Interactive (http://www.cnn.com)
Updated frequently by Cable Network News, this site spotlights the latest headlines and news, offers in-depth analysis of specialized issues such as the environment, and provides live streaming audio of CNN broadcasts.

Ecola (http://www.ecola.com/news)
Track the news in a particular city in the United States or in another country by locating a local newspaper or magazine's Web site on the Ecola Newsstand site. As a special feature, this site locates publications with online searchable archives.

International Herald Tribune (http://www.iht.com/IHT/home.html)
Read the latest global news—posted daily, Monday through Saturday—covering top headlines, financial markets, technology, and special features.

New York Times (http://www.nytimes.com)
On the home page, you can click to access news headlines updated every ten minutes or hear a brief audio news program updated twice every hour. In addition to reading the day's top news, you can go to the "Business" section (once you register and obtain a free password) to see the latest business stories.

Online U.S. News & World Report (http://www.usnews.com/usnews/main.htm)
News and analysis from *U.S. News and World Report*, covering both domestic and global events. A special feature is the magazine's ranking of colleges and graduate schools.

Time Warner's Pathfinder Network (http://www.pathfinder.com)
Time Warner offers access to all its media on a single giant site, so you can simply click to see news stories (from *Time*), scan today's top headlines and photos (*Time Daily*), read business articles (from *Fortune*), read about business in Asia (*AsiaWeek*), and more.

USA Today (http://www.usatoday.com)
The online version of *USA Today* presents daily headlines, business news, personal finance information, and a searchable news archive with articles from 1987 to the present.

Current Business News

For up-to-the-minute information about specific industries and companies, business trends, and financial market activity, point your Web browser to the following sites:

American City Business Journals (http://www.amcity.com)
Dozens of business newspapers are linked to this site, where you can search for relevant business articles by city, industry, or company name.

Bloomberg Business News (http://www.bloomberg.com)
Scan the business headlines, look at world news, see how the financial markets are performing, and access Bloomberg television and radio coverage at this Web site.

Business Week Online (http://www.businessweek.com)
Here, you can read articles from the latest weekly issue or, for a fee, retrieve older articles from *Business Week's* archives. Registration required to access selected articles.

CNN Financial (http://www.cnnfn.com/index.html)
In addition to stock quotes and a search facility for locating financial information, this site offers access to news, analysis, and in-depth coverage of political issues in Washington and other world capitals.

Fast Company (http://www.fastcompany.com)
This ever-changing site features in-depth articles on management, case studies of successful companies, interviews with experts, and extensive coverage of leading-edge issues and technologies.

Forbes (http://www.forbes.com)
Look at the table of contents from the latest issue of this business magazine, or locate archived articles about management, startups, companies, electronic commerce, and much more.

Inc. Online (http://www.inc.com)
The editors of *Inc.* magazine present articles about entrepreunerial businesses, offer management tips, look into peer-to-peer networking, answer questions about business subjects, profile startups, and review technology.

MSNBC (http://www.msnbc.com/news/COM_front.asp)
Microsoft and NBC have teamed up to provide late-breaking news about business, finance, technology, and science, plus live multimedia coverage of key events in business and industry.

USA Today Money (http://www.usatoday.com/money/mfront.htm)
Read today's business headlines, check the financial markets, and gain insights into important personal and professional financial issues—all at this well-organized site.

Wall Street Journal (http://www.wsj.com)
Subscription-based interactive version of this authoritative business newspaper. Free areas include: top business news (in English, Spanish, and Portuguese), career information, small business services for entrepreneurs, and an annual report ordering service.

Your Turn

Launch your Web browser and move to the Dow Jones Business Directory (http://businessdirectory.dowjones.com). This directory rates sites on the basis of content, speed, navigation, and design. Using the search facility, look for sites about management.

How do the brief descriptions, coupled with the ratings scores, help you decide which links to explore?
Which sites would you visit if you were starting a small business?
Which sites would you visit if you were researching a class project about corporate management?

Management Topics

In addition to tracking general news and business trends, managers need to be aware of developments in specific management disciplines. Depending on the management courses you are taking—and the career path you are planning—you will want to bookmark the appropriate Internet sites from the following seven disciplines.

General Management

Access Business Online (http://www.clickit.com/touch/home.htm)
This site is a gateway to business publications and offers links to legal and regulatory data, financial information, executive jobs, world trade, and other resources for managers.

American Society for Quality (http://www.asqc.org/)
Locate information about ISO 9000 and ISO 14000 international quality standards on this site, which also features information about quality conferences, books, and publications.

Center for Corporate Community Relations (http://www.bc.edu/bc_org/avp/csom/cccr)
Based at Boston College, this site presents journal articles about relations between business and community. Also on this site: information about conferences, newsletters, and online forums for idea interchange.

Department of the Navy Total Quality Leadership Office (http://tql-navy.org/)
This U.S. government site features a range of quality management resources, including information about education and training, implementation, assessment and performance review, newsletter articles, and much more.

Dilbert (http://www.unitedmedia.com/comics/dilbert)
When you need a laugh—or a flash of pointed insight into corporate life—visit Scott Adams' Dilbert comic strip, which tickles the funny bone with barbs from the world of cubicle dwellers.

Hoovers Online (http://www.hoovers.com)
You can obtain brief company descriptions free at this site and follow links to recent articles about the company as well as to the firm's Web site; more comprehensive company reports are available for a fee.

National Quality Institute (http://www.quality.nist.gov/)
Home of the Malcolm Baldrige National Quality Award, this site features a quality library, showcases the stories of recent award winners, and explains how to apply for this prestigious quality award.

Sloan Management Review (http://web.mit.edu/smr-online/)
Read the latest journal articles about management issues and browse information from past issues as well.

Work Family Life Interactions (http://www.cyfc.umn.edu/work.html)
The University of Minnesota hosts this site, which contains an extensive bibliography about work and family issues, a summary of research, selected speeches, newsletters, and coverage of legal issues.

Organizational Behavior
Behavior Online (http://www.behavior.net)
Developed for mental health and applied behavioral science professionals, this site presents moderated conversation threads of ongoing discussions about key OB issues. There are links to related sites and information about OB books and resources.

Center for the Study of Work Teams (http://www.workteams.unt.edu)
Based at the University of North Texas, this site hosts the TeamNet e-mail list for ongoing discussion of team issues. You can also join the forum for discussion of teams in the workplace and read newsletter articles about current concepts and trends.

Diversity Training Group (http://www.diversitydtg.com)
Read through FAQs on diversity issues, diversity training, sexual harassment, and related issues at this site, which also features case studies of companies addressing diversity concerns.

Knowledge Management and Organizational Learning (http://www.brint.com/OrgLrng.htm)
Here, you can access an extensive set of resources about knowledge management issues, including academic papers, books and bibliographies, business publication articles, and links to sites about organizational learning, information systems, and more.

Organization Development Network (http://www.tmn.com/odn/index.html)
This site features many resources to support organization development activities, including a listing of e-mail discussion groups, events calendar, directory of practitioners, and links to related organizations.

Personality Typing Systems (http://www.sunsite.unc.edu/personality)
Questions, answers, and discussion threads from discussions on personality typing systems, drawn from the newsgroup alt.psychology.personality.

Self-directed Work Teams (http://users.ids.net/~brim/sdwtt.html)
Click your way through the giant list of links to case studies, examples, studies, bibliographies, and other resources related to work teams in business and government organizations.

Team Management Systems (http://www.tms.com.au/welcome.html)
At this site, you can access a variety of resources about work teams, including training tips, discussion group forums, articles, case studies, books, and more.

University of Texas - Austin (http://www.bus.utexas.edu/kman)
Explore knowledge management and business applications at this site, which presents FAQs about knowledge management, a useful glossary, numerous case studies, and other resources.

Your Turn

Launch your Web browser and go to the Keirsey Character Sorter (http://keirsey.com/cgi-bin/keirsey/kcs.cgi), an online version of a personality test (similar to the Myers-Briggs test). Click on the link to read about the test and then answer the questions.

What do the results tell you about yourself and the type of organizational member you are likely to be?

Human Resource Management

Benefits Link (http://www.benefitslink.com)
Visit this site for expert advice about benefits issues. In addition to links to data about employee benefits regulations and government documents, you can look at job openings and job-wanted listings, read benefits newsletters, and search for other valuable resources.

Equal Employment Opportunity Commission (http://www.eeoc.gov)
Check this U.S. government site for information about equal employment opportunity regulations, enforcement, discrimination, assistance, and small business information.

Foundation for Enterprise Development (http://www.fed.org/)
At this site, you will find a wealth of information devoted to equity compensation programs for employee and management motivation, including a library of related Internet links.

International Association for Human Resource Information Management (http://www.ihrim.org)
A good site for identifying global resources, finding jobs or networking with other professionals, locating listservs, and following links to related sites.

Ray's List of HRM Connections (http://www.nbs.ntu.ac.uk/staff/lyerj/hrm_link.htm)
Based at the Nottingham Business School in the United Kingdom, this site features a comprehensive categorized listing of links for many HR topics, including employee relations, business psychology, telecommuting, online HR courses, and much more.

School of Industrial and Labor Relations at Cornell University (http://www.ilr.cornell.edu/workplace.html)
Here, you can search and download archived documents on various HR topics such as the glass ceiling and child labor laws. Also look through the links to centers and groups that focus on labor relations (see Figure 6.2).

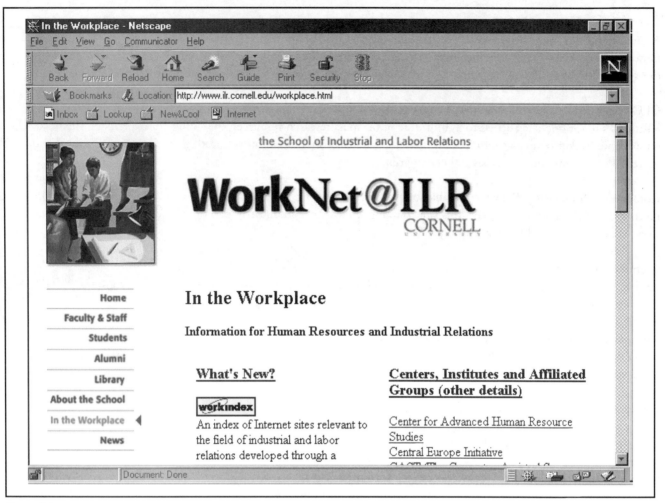

Figure 6.2. The School of Industrial and Labor Relations Workplace at Cornell University offers on its site a wide range of human resource management articles and links to topics on labor relations.

Society for Human Resource Management (http://www.shrm.org)
This comprehensive Web site features articles from HR Magazine, news articles, conferences, white papers, updates of state laws affecting HRM, and an unusually wide variety of links to sources of information about human resources.

Training and Development Home Page (http://www.tcm.com/trdev)
Visiting this site, you will find an extensive listing of links to sites focusing on human resource development principles and applications.

TrainingNet (http://www.trainingnet.com/)
Register at this site to participate in teleconferences about human resource development and training issues. Also, check here for news articles about employee and management training programs.

For more information about employee benefits, you can subscribe to the Benefits-L listserv by contacting Listproc@frank.mtsu.edu. To stay updated on pension policy issues such as tax implications, you can subscribe to the pension-policy listserv by contacting erisa@benefitslink.com.

Strategic Management

Annual Report Gallery (http://www.reportgallery.com)
Download and read through financial reports posted by many U.S., Japanese, and South Korean firms. Special sections highlight exceptionally attractive reports and the reports of corporations with outstanding financial results.

CEO Express (http://www.ceoexpress.com)
Visit this site for one-click access to a multitude of business research resources, including company data, financial quotes and market results, government agency sites, international news sources, leading business publications, and more data for competitive analysis or benchmarking.

Companies Online (http://www.companiesonline.com)
From Dun & Bradstreet and Lycos, this site contains reports on 100,000 companies, including ownership, executives, ticker symbol, and links to corporate Web sites.

Competitive Intelligence Guide (http://www.fuld.com)
Fuld & Company presents techniques and resources for researching competitive activities, including links to industry association Web sites, trade shows, industry reference materials, and a question/answer feature.

Corporate Financials Online (http://www.cfonews.com)
If you want to find out about the condition of your competitors, check this site for an alphabetical listing of selected financial reports. Also look at financial market snapshots, business headlines, and summaries of financial market results.

Corporate Governance (http://www.corpgov.net)
Read about corporate governance and shareholder involvement, using this site's library and links to annotated articles, books, book reviews, speeches, and journal publications.

Corporate Information (http://www.corporateinformation.com)
This is a very convenient site for locating information about public and private companies all over the world, because entries are organized according to country.

Fedstats (http://www.fedstats.gov)
Maintained by the U.S. government, this site makes available mountains of statistical data from 70 federal agencies, including the Environmental Protection Agency, the Internal Revenue Service, and the Agency for International Development. As you evaluate your company's environment, you can search for relevant statistics according to agency, subject (such as agriculture or labor), or region.

Your Turn

Access the home page for Franklin Covey (http://www.covey.com/whatshot/).
Use the site map or the search facility to locate the mission statement builder and create your personal mission statement.

What is the benefit of having a personal mission statement?
How does such a statement differ from a business mission statement?

Small Business and Entrepreneurship

Consumer Information Catalog Small Business Publications (http://www.pueblo.gsa.gov/smbuss.htm)
This site lists free and low-cost U.S. government publications available to help small business owners, such as booklets about Small Business Administration financing.

EntrepreNet (http://www.enterprise.org)
Here at the Entrepreneur's Electronic Resource Center, you will find links to newsletters offering advice, venture capital sources, newsletters, conferences, and continuing education courses for small business owners.

Entrepreneur Magazine's Small Business Square (http://www.entrepreneurmag.com)
Check this site for FAQs on small business problems, articles by and for entrepreneurs, information about software for startups, and links to magazines about international entrepreneurship.

eWeb (http://www.slu.edu/eweb)
From Saint Louis University, this site offers resources for establishing, operating, and growing your own business. Search the bibliographies and the how-to sections for detailed instructions; also look through the links to related organizations.

Idea Café (http://www.ideacafe.com)
For practical advice, articles, and answers to questions about running a small business, visit this site, which also includes links to related sources and to Dilbert cartoons.

Industry Canada Strategis Information Site (http://strategis.ic.gc.ca)
For Canadian entrepreneurs, this government site offers one-stop assistance with information about how to do business in the country. It also contains links to various government agencies.

Ozemail (http://www.ozemail.com.au/internet/business/index.html)
Visit this Australian site for international links to resources for small businesses, including suggested readings, jobs, Internet tutorials, international stock news, and more.

SCORE (http://www.score.org)
The nonprofit Service Corps of Retired Executives maintains this site to help entrepreneurs deal with the challenges of starting and running a small business. In addition, you can locate nearby small business workshops, receive free e-mail business counseling, scan small business FAQs, and find more small business resources.

Small Business Journal (http://www.tsbj.com/)
Read through articles in current and back issues of this magazine to learn more about strategies and tactics for successfully operating your own business.

Small Business Resource Center (http://www.webcom.com/seaquest/sbrc/welcome.html)
This site invites visitors to read free how-to reports about business plans, franchising, home businesses, and other critical issues for new businesses. Also check the links to related sites.

U.S. Copyright Office (http://lcweb.loc.gov/copyright)
New businesses need to understand how to protect their intellectual property. This site provides forms, rules, and updated information about filing and protecting copyrights.

U.S. Small Business Administration (http://www.sbaonline.sba.gov)
You can access information about starting, financing, and expanding a small business at this site, which also includes
links to outside resources such as trade shows and international trade opportunities (see Figure 6.3).

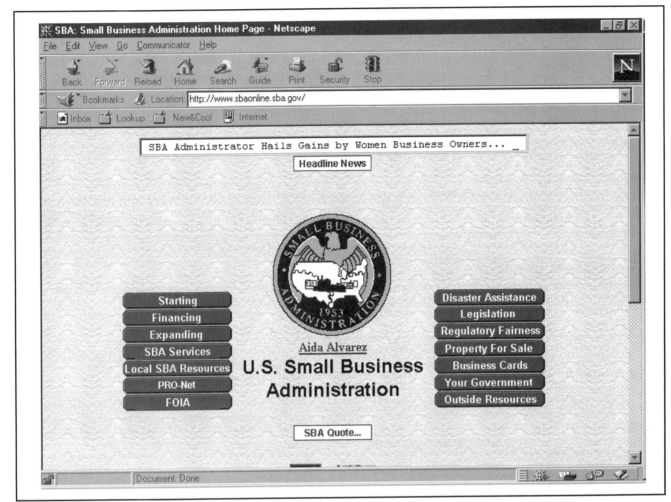

Figure 6.3. The U.S. Small Business Administration offers information on the many aspects of running a small business and can also link you to domestic and international resources.

Yahoo's Business & Economy: Small Business Information (http://www.yahoo.com)
Check here for listings of the day's online chats and programs related to small business issues. This section also lists
directories, conferences, awards, publications, venture capital sources, and other useful links for entrepreneurs.

International Business and Management

Asian Business News Interactive (http://www.abn.com.sg/)
Here, you'll find the latest business news and financial market performance for Asian countries, provided by NBC
and Dow Jones.

Asia Inc. Online (http://www.asia-inc.com)
Search financial news and archived articles from 1994 to today, covering business activities such as mergers and acquisitions, the Asian economic environment, and other key facts that can influence corporate performance.

Association of Southeast Asian Nations (http://www.asean.or.jp/emenu.html)
This site offers information to support trade and tourism in ASEAN member countries, including Indonesia, Japan, Malaysia, Philippines, Singapore, Thailand, and Brunei Darussalam.

Canadian Government site (http://canada.gc.ca/main_e.html)
The home page for Canadian government information, departments and agencies, services, and links to provincial and territorial government sites (available in English or French).

European Business News Interactive (http://www.cnbceurope.com)
This is the European counterpart of the NBC/Dow Jones Asian Business News site, covering industry and company headlines as well as current financial results and live broadcasts.

European Union (http://www.europa.eu.int/)
Choose the language in which you want to read the latest news about European Union events, statistics, publications, databases, and policies.

Foreign Exchange Rates (http://cnnfn.com/markets/currencies.html)
Up-to-the-minute exchange rates for the world's currencies are posted on this CNN Financial News Web site.

Global Business Centre (http://www.euromktg.com/gbc/)
A handy collection of links to international resources in English and in other languages in categories such as business, culture, jobs, and online publications. You can also search for specific key words or names on this site.

International Business Directory (http://www.ntu.ac.sg/ntu/lib/doing.htm)
This Web site, maintained by Nanyang Technological University Library in Singapore, should be bookmarked by anyone involved in world trade. It boasts an exhaustive set of links to resources, alphabetized by region.

International Business Resources (http://ciber.bus.msu.edu/busres.htm)
From the Michigan State University Center for International Business and Research, this site invites visitors to search by keyword or browse the index for journal articles, country-specific data, international trade information, and many other topics.

NAFTA Border Home Page (http://www.iep.doc.gov/border/nafta.htm)
At this U.S. government site, you will find links to many documents and resources related to the North American Free Trade Agreement, including university sites, government home pages, and much more.

Statistics Bureau and Statistics Center of Japan (http://www.stat.go.jp)
If you need official demographic or economic statistics about Japan, look at the facts and figures available at this site, which is available in English or Japanese.

Virtual International Business and Economic Sources
(http://www.uncc.edu/lis/library/reference/intbus/vibehome.htm)

Here is an extensive set of links, set up by the University of North Carolina at Charlotte, leading to resources about international business. Links are organized by region, country, and general topics such as trade issues, patents, energy, and taxation.

World Fact Book (http://www.odci.gov/cia/publications/factbook/index.htm)
From the Central Intelligence Agency, this comprehensive site offers searchable, downloadable information organized by topic and region. If you want to find out about a country's economy, government, infrastructure, or communication—or see a map—be sure to bookmark this site (see Figure 6.4).

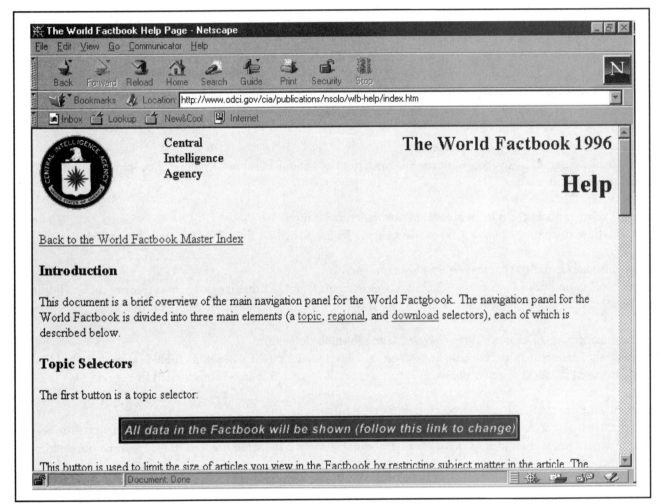

Figure 6.4. The World Fact Book, developed by the Central Intelligence Agency, is a great place to start gathering information on a wealth of international topics.

Ethics and Social Responsibility

Center for the Advancement of Ethics (http://www.uwyo.edu/a&s/phil/cae/dir.htm)
This site, based at the University of Wyoming, features essays on ethical issues, codes of ethics, and notices of conferences.

Corporate Citizenship Resource Center (http://ttrcnew.ttrc.doleta.gov/citizen)
From the U.S. Department of Labor, this site offers principles for corporate citizenship plus profiles of companies committed to these principles. In addition, the site posts speeches by U.S. officials, selected quotes, and links to related sites.

Illinois Institute of Technology Center for the Study of Ethics in the Professions (http://www.iit.edu/departments/csep/)
Use the online library at this site to review any of 850 codes of ethics on file. Also read through ethics essays and discussions of issues such as whistleblowing.

Institute for Business and Professional Ethics (http://www.depaul.edu/ethics)
Based at DePaul University, this comprehensive site hosts the *Online Journal of Ethics*, a newsletter, conference listings, and numerous links to other online resources about business ethics.

Cornell Work & Environment Initiative (http://www.cfe.cornell.edu/wei)
Based at Cornell University, this Web site offers information about bringing together management, labor, environmental, and government leaders to foster a positive connection between the economy and the environment. There are many useful links to related sites.

Your Turn

The ethical standards that shape employee behavior are crucial to every organization. Visit the Ethics Connection Web site (http://www.scu.edu/ethics/homepage.shtml), maintained by the Markkula Center for Applied Ethics at Santa Clara University. Read through one of the case studies and examine the comments posted by other visitors.

Do you agree or disagree with the comments? Why?
Post your own comments about this case, supporting your ideas with what you have learned about ethics in your management courses.

Managing Your Management Career

Earlier in this guide, you learned about the many Web sites you can use to research occupations, investigate potential employers, locate job openings, and submit your résumé to databanks. This section lists just a few of the Internet sites where you will find practical ideas for starting and developing your career in management.

Business Job Finder (http://www.cob.ohio-state.edu/dept/~fin/osujobs.htm)
Although this Ohio State University site offers many job-search features, it also offers career guides to several management specialties plus guides to other business careers.

Career Action Center (http://www.careeraction.org)
Check this site for advice about career self-reliance and management and useful links to other career development resources on the Internet.

Career Assessment Tools (http://www.jobweb.org/catapult/Assess.htm)
From Job Web, this site links to a collection of career assessment tools, including sites about career development and sites offering online self-tests for career planning.

Career Babe (http://www.careerbabe.com/index.html)
Not for women only, this site offers contains a question-and-answer area for career advice, links to other career development sites, and features such as suggestions for what to do when your job goes away.

HR Plaza (http://www.hrplaza.com/hrcareercenter/gowhere/)
Visit this site for advice on career management for human resource professionals, along with a changing assortment of featured articles about careers in the field.

Monster HR (http://www.monsterhr.com/)
The people who run the Monster Board created this special area devoted to developing a career in human resources, with articles and advice for managers at all stages of their careers.

U.S. News & World Report Career Guide (http://www.usnews.com/usnews/edu/beyond/bccguide.htm)
At this site, you will find special features about career planning and development plus articles about issues such as the glass ceiling and work productivity.

Your Turn

Visit at least two of the career sites listed above and look for advice about managing your career in management.

Based on this information, what steps can you take at the start of your career to be prepared for more responsibility in higher management positions or to develop the management skills you need to run your own business?

The Internet as a Management Learning Tool

Now that you are familiar with the variety of management resources available on the Internet, you are ready to tap these resources to hone your management skills. In the following assignment, you assume the role of a management professional who must combine the information-gathering tools of the Internet with management concepts to solve a typical business problem. To start, launch your Web browser and move onto the Internet—then follow this exercise, step by step, all the way through to the end.

Your Assignment

One of the most critical challenges facing managers in any business is the choice of competitive strategy. In this assignment, you are a strategic planner working for Amazon.com, a fast-growing retailer that uses the Internet, rather than a network of stores, to sell books to customers worldwide.

Jeff Bezos, the company's founder, has asked you to (1) conduct an environmental scan to understand the company's competitive situation and then, based on this information, (2) suggest an appropriate competitive strategy for continued success. Your report is due in 24 hours.

Gathering Data

Your first task is to determine who Amazon.com's competitors are. Using online sources of industry information, identify other companies that are retailing books on the Internet. Next, search the Web to learn all you can about your company and each competitor, including sales, profitability, specialties, pricing, promotions, market share, and financial condition. What do industry analysts and business publications say about Amazon.com and its competitors?

What public statements have rival executives made about their future goals and plans?
To put all this competitive data into perspective, you'll need to find out how the book market is faring: Are overall book sales growing, shrinking, or remaining stable? How much of the overall market has Internet-based book retailing been able to snag—and what are the projections for growth in cyberspace book sales?

As you scour the Web for the information you need, remember that each search tool, database, and directory operates slightly differently from the others. Therefore, you will want to use many different sites in the course of collecting your data.

Analysis

After you have gathered data on the market, your competitors, and Amazon.com, you need to analyze this information and summarize your conclusions. First, lay out what each competitor is doing and compare this to what your company is doing. Which companies are growing their market share (and which are not)? How well is each company doing in terms of sales, profits, and financial strength? Which firms have recently announced or undertaken aggressive promotions or other major marketing actions? Which firms specialize in certain book categories and which compete across the board with Amazon.com?

Now evaluate the current and future potential of the online book market. Is growth expected—or will competitors be battling to take share from each other in a stable or shrinking market? What market pitfalls and opportunities might benefit each player in the market? How well do you think Amazon.com and its competitors are positioned for the coming years?

Implications for Your Company

Using the Porter model of competitive strategies or another model, determine the type of competitive strategy that Amazon.com and each rival appears to be implementing. Prepare a matrix for each company in the market, showing how its actions and results fit its competitive strategy. Include a column on each matrix to indicate your assessment of the strength or weakness of each competitor's strategy, given the situation in the overall book market.

On the basis of these matrices, draft a report highlighting Amazon.com's competitive advantage. Include specific steps your company might take to counter each competitor and gain market share in the next few years. Take a few minutes to put yourself in the place of your competitors and consider what response they might have to your suggested actions. What can you do to preempt or diffuse these competitive reactions?

Draft a brief report to summarize the data and your conclusions for Jeff Bezos' review. Be sure that your analysis and recommendations are consistent with the data and with sound management principles. Remember, the future success of your company will depend, in part, on decisions that are made as a result of your work.

Summary

What have you learned from this assignment? First, you have gained first-hand knowledge of the Internet as a convenient, speedy source of raw data. Instead of searching through stacks of reference books and reports at the library, you simply keyed in the appropriate Internet addresses and then read through files or printed out details as needed. Second, you have seen that the Internet is a learning *tool*, not a substitute for learning. As a manager, it is up to *you* to evaluate and interpret the data you gather from the Internet so you can use it to support better decisions for your company.

Appendix I:
Business-related
Internet Addresses

As this booklet explains, once you're on the Internet, you can travel the globe. To get started, try the addresses that follow. They're grouped in various categories, but any one address may lead you to some totally unexpected sites. Experiment!

For information on our educational publications, in business, try the Prentice Hall Web site:
http://www.prenhall.com/phbusiness

	Site Name/Sponsor	Information	Address
Accounting	Rutgers University	Accounting education information	http://www.rutgers.edu/accounting/raw.html
	Edgar	Database of corporate information.	http://www.sec.gov/edgarhp.htm
	Edgar-Online	Up-to-the-minute corporate news.	http://www.edgar-online.com/
	Professional Accounting	Springboard for locating many	
	Organizations	accounting organizations.	http://www.bus.orst.edu/
	American Accounting Association	Accounting education.	http://www.rutgers.edu/Accounting/raw/aaa/aaa.htm
	American Institute of Certified Public		http://www.rutgers.edu/Accounting/raw/aicpa/home.htm
	Accountants		
	Institute of Management Accountants		http://panoptic.csustan.edu/ima/imafront.htm
	Accounting Companies/Organizations		http://www.library.ualberta.ca/library_html/subjects/account ing/links_accounting.htm
Businesses	IBM		http://www.ibm.com
(Home Pages)	Charles Schwab & Co.		http://www.schwab.com
	GE Information Services		http://www.geis.com
	Texas Instruments		http://www.ti.com
	American Century Investments		http://www.americancentury.com
	Toyota		http://www.toyota.com
	Zenith Data Systems		http://www.zds.com
	3M Innovation Network		http://www.mmm.com
	Aetna		http://www.aetna.com
	American Stock Exchange		http://www.amex.com
	Ameritech		http://www.ameritech.com
	AT&T		http://www.att.com/
	Bell Atlantic		http://www.bell-atl.com
	Canon		http://www.usa.canon.com
	Chrysler		http://www.chryslercorp.com
	Compaq		http://www.compaq.com
	Federal Express		http://www.fedex.com/
	Ford		http://www.ford.com
	Hewlett-Packard		http://www.hp.com
	Kodak		http://www.kodak.com
	Eli Lilly & Co.		http://www.lilly.com
	Lotus		http://www.lotus.com
	MCI		http://www.mci.com
	Microsoft		http://www.microsoft.com
	Motorola		http://www.mot.com
	Novell		http://www.novell.com
	Raytheon		http://www.raytheon.com
	Siemens		http://www.siemens.com
	Sun Microsystems		http://www.sun.com
	Unisys		http://www.unisys.com
	UPS		http://www.ups.com
Business Law	Legal Information Institute		http://www.law.cornell.edu/supct.
	Supreme Court		http://supct.law.cornell.edu/
	PH BLAW		http://www.prenhall.com/phblaw
	Ray August - Professor of Business Law		http://www.wsu.edu:8080/~august

Category	Resource	Description	URL
	ABA Lawlink	ABA legal research selected starting points	http://www.abanet.org/lawlink/home.html
	Law Resources on the Internet		http://www.rbvdnr.com/lawres.htm
	Academy of Legal Studies in Business		http://miavx1.acs.muohio.edu/%7Eherrondj/
Business Publications	Inc. Magazine		http://www.inc.com
	Dow Jones	Access to the publisher of The Wall Street Journal	http://bis.dowjones.com
	Electronic newsstand	A long list includes business publications.	http://www.enews.com
Business Statistics	SPSS	Statistical product and service solutions.	http://www.spss.com
	Statistics on the Web	Various statistical resources.	http://www.execpc.com/~helberg/statistics.html
	Basic Sources of Economic Statistics		http://www.princeton.edu/~econlib/basic.html
	A Guide to Statistical Computing Resourceson the Internet		http://asa.ugl.lib.umich.edu/chdocs/statistics/stat_guide_home.html
Finance/ Economics	Woodrow	Has a wide variety of financial information about banking, etc.; sponsored by Federal Reserve Bank of Minneapolis	http://woodrow.mpls.frb.fed.us
	Edgar	Database of corporate information.	http://www.sec.gov/edgarhp.htm
	Dun & Bradstreet Credit Information		http://www.dnb.com
	Money Magazine Personal Finance Center		http://www.pathfinder.com/money
	Corporate Finance Network		http://www.corpfinet.com
	Hoovers Online		http://www.hoovers.com
	The U.S. Tax Code Online		http://www.fourmilab.ch/ustax/ustax.html
	PC Quote		http://www.pcquote.com
	Investor Web		http://www.investorweb.com/
	MIT Stock Master		http://www.stockmaster.com
	Chicago Mercantile Exchange		http://www.cme.com/index.html
	The Syndicate		http://www.moneypages.com/syndicate/
	FinanceNet	Financial Management in Business	http://www.financenet.gov/
	Wall Street Journal Money & Investing Update		http://update.wsj.com/
General Reference	Webster's Dictionary		http://www.m-w.com/dictionary.htm
	List of American Universities		http://www.clas.ufl.edu/CLAS/american-universities.html
	AT&T Toll-Free Number Directory		http://att.net/dir800/
	CNN Financial Network Reference Desk		http:cnnfn.com/researchit/referencedesk/
	Listing of associations on the WWW		http://www.asaenet.org/Gateway/OnlineAssocSlist.html
	Better Business Bureau	Directory, national information.	http://www.bbb.org
	The List	List of 5,023 Internet service providers	http://thelist.iworld.com/
	Mondaq Business Briefing		http://www.mondaq.com
	Dun & Bradstreet	Data on millions of U.S. companies.	http://www.dnb.com
Government Resources	Library of Congress	A premier research library	http://lcweb.loc.gov/homepage/lchp.html
	National Technology Transfer Center	Connects private sector business with Federal lab system.	http://iridium.nttc.edu/nttc.html
	U.S. Patent and Trademark Office		http://www.uspto.gov
	Commerce Information Locator Service	Access to Department of Commerce databases.	http://www.doc.gov
	F.E.D. Resource Library		http://www.fed.org/library/index.html
	Central Intelligence Agency	Access to CIA World Factbook.	http://www.odci.gov
	Census Bureau	Social and economic indicators.	http://www.census.gov
Human Resources	HR Professional's Gateway to the Internet	Eric Wilson's home page, contains numerous HR-related Internet links.	http://www.wp.com/mike-shelley/
	AFL-CIO	Home page of the AFL-CIO, a labor federation to which most U.S. labor unions belong.	http://www.aflcio.org/
	American Compensation Association	Home page of the American Compensation Association, an organization of professionals engaged in the design, implementation, and management of employee compensation programs.	http://www.acaonline.org/
	Americans with Disabilities Act (ADA) Document Center	Provides numerous links to ADA resources, including sites regarding such specific disabilities as cancer, hearing impairment, and alcohol and drug-related illnesses.	http://janweb.icdi.wvu.edu/kinder/
	Benefits Link	Provides information on a wide variety of employee benefits plans.	http://www.benefitslink.com/index.shtml
	Career Mosaic	Contains a wealth of career and job information, including a large database of current job opportunities.	http://www.careermosaic.com/
	HR Magazine	Articles form HR Magazine, published monthly by the Society for Human Resource Management.	http://www.shrm.org/docs/Hrmagazine.html
	Training Net	An information resource for those interested in training issues.	http://trainingnet.com/
	Thunderbird School of International Management	Provides access to outstanding sources of international business and HR information.	http://www.t-bird.edu/
Management	Institute of Management & Administration		http://www.ioma.com
	Academy of Management		http://www.aom.pace.edu
	Small Business Administration		http://www.sbaonline.sba.gov/

Marketing	U.S. Department of Commerce Information Service		http://www.doc.gov
	International Institute for Management Development	A focus on executive development from an international perspective.	http://www.imd.ch/
	U.S. Census Bureau	Has data on demographics from the U.S. census	http://www.census.gov
	American Demographics Magazine		http://www.marketingtools.com
	Nielsen Media Research	Nielsen contains perhaps the most authoritative study on Internet demographics.. The study follows the most reliable methodology for obtaining a random and representative population sample.	http://www.nielsen.com
	SRI - Stanford Research Institute	The Stanford Research Institute provides some of the best psychographic research on Web users. The site allows you to determine you own VALS and iVALS type.	http://future.sri.com
	Advertising Age	Madison Avenue's daily news and account changes for the industry's two news sources. Online access to new media and marketing coverage from Interactive Media & Marketing.	http://www.adage.com/
	Adweek Online	Site includes article archives from Adweek, Brandweek, and Mediaweek - and access to Adweek databases, such as Accounts I Review and Adweek's Client/Brand directory.	http://www.adweek.com/
	American Association of Advertising		http://www.commercepark.com/AAAA/
Operations Management	Web Digest for Marketers		http://wdfm.com/
	Operations Management Index		http://www.wbs.warwick.ac.uk/omindex/bib/
	Operations Research/Management Science	A focus on decision/risk analysis.	http://www.lumina.com/DA/
	Operations Research	Wide range of newsgroups, discussion groups, papers, and more.	http://www.rrz.uni-koeln.de/themen/or/
	Network Resources for Operations Research		http://mat.gsia.cmu.edu/resource.html
Org. Behavior	The Keirsey Temperament Sorter	Understand your personality and how it shapes your behavior	http://www.keirsey.com/cgi-bin/keirsey/newkts.cgi
	Entrepreneur Magazine	A wealth of information for aspiring entrepreneurs and small business managers.	http://www.entrepreneurmag.com/
	The Business Process Reengineering Online Learning Center	An excellent source for articles and reviews, book abstracts, mailing lists and forums, and reference lists and Web sites related to reengineering and business process reengineering teams.	http://www.prosci.com/index.htm
	Psychology Centre	Learn to distinguish between reinforcing and nonreinforcing consequences in complexorganizational situations.	http://server.bmod.athabascau.ca/html/prtut/reinpair.htm
Small Business Mgmt	Small Business Administration		http://www.sbaonline.sba.gov
	FranNet	General franchiser information.	http://www.frannet.com
	American Individual Magazine & Coffeehouse		http://aimc.com/aimc/
	Institute of Management and Administration	Links to hundreds of business sites.	http://www.ioma.com/index.html
	Franchise Handbook Online	Franchising opportunities.	http://www.franchise1.com/
	National Small Business Development Center	Small business and entrepreneurial opportunities.	http://www.smallbiz.suny.edu/
	Research Network		
	World M&A Network	Companies for sale, merger candidates.	http://www.worldm-anetwork.com/
	Resources for the Entrepreneur		http://www.DraperVC.com/Resources.html
Student Success	Tripod	Wide variety of educational and career resources for students, including online resume service and database	http://www.tripod.com
	JobTrak	Online resume and recruitment service; posts over 500 new job listings a day	http://www.jobtrak.com
	"Best Bets from the Net"	Lists the best sites for career hunting; maintained and created by two professors from the University of Michigan.	http://www.lib.umich.edu/
	Career Magazine	Online magazine that sponsors moderate career forums	http://www.careermag.com
	The Accounting.com Home Page	Source for employment opportunities in finance	http://www.accounting.com
	Job Hunter		http://www.collegegrad.com/
	Occupational Outlook Handbook		http://stats.bls.gov:80/ocohome.htm
	America's Job Bank	List of all the government jobs available in U.S. State Employment Offices	http://www.ajb.dni.us/

Appendix II
Glossary

Background
This refers to an image or color that is present in the background of a viewed Web document. Complex images are becoming very popular as backgrounds but require a great deal more time to download. The color of default background can be set for most Web browsers.

Bookmark
This refers to a list of URLs saved within a browser. The user can edit and modify the bookmark list to add and delete URLs as the user's interests change. Bookmark is a term used by Netscape to refer to the user's list of URLs; Hotlist is used by Mosaic for the same purpose. (See Hotlist, Mosaic, and URL.)

Browser
A browser is a software program that runs on a personal computer and provides a graphical user interface (GUI) to the Web. The two most popular browsers are Netscape Navigator (or Communicator) and Microsoft Internet Explorer.

Bulletin Board Service
This is an electronic bulletin board. It is sometimes referred to as a BBS. Information on a BBS is posted to a computer where people can access, read, and comment on it. A BBS may or may not be connected to the Internet. Some are accessible by modem dial-in only.

Chat room
This is a site that allows for real-time person-to-person interactions.

Clickable image (Clickable map)
This refers to an interface used in Web documents that allow the user to click, or select, different areas of an image and receive different responses. Clickable images are becoming a popular way to offer a user many different selections within a common visual format.

Client
This is a software program used to view information from remote computers. Clients function in a Client-Server information exchange model. This term may also be loosely applied to the computer that is used to request information from the server. (See Server.)

Compressed file
This refers to a file or document that has been compacted to save memory space so that it can be easily and quickly transferred through the Internet.

Cyberspace
Cyberspace is used to describe the environment which users enter into on the Net.

Download
This is the process of transferring a file, document, or program from a remote computer to a local computer. (See Upload.)

Domain Name
Domain names are used to address sites on the Internet. The top-level domain names are com, edu, gov, net, and org. Second level domain names usually correspond to familiar trademarks like Coca-Cola, McDonalds, Pepsi, etc.

E-mail	This is the short name for electronic mail. E-mail is sent electronically from one person to another. Some companies have e-mail systems that are not part of the Internet. E-mail can be sent to one person or to many different people. (I sometimes refer to this as Junk E-mail.)
Ethernet	Ethernet refers to the most popular transport technology standard used in local area networks (LANs).
FAQ	Frequently Asked Questions (FAQs) often appear as a link on the home pages of different sites.
Frame Relay	Frame Relay refers to the most popular transport technology standard used in wide area networks (WANs).
Forms	This refers to an interface element used within Web documents to allow the user to send information back to a Web server. With a forms interface, the user is requested to type responses within entry windows to be returned to the server for processing. Forms rely on a server computer to process the submittals. They are becoming more common as browser and server software improve.
GUI	Is an acronym for Graphical User Interface. It is a combination of the appearance and the method of interacting with a computer. A GUI requires the use of a mouse to select commands on an icon-based monitor screen. Macintosh and Windows operating systems are examples of typical GUIs.
Helper	This is software that is used to help a browser view information formats that it couldn't normally view.
Home Page	A Home Page is first page that you see when you visit a site (e.g., www.honda.com). Sites often have many different home pages if they host many different users. In this case you must know the subdirectory where the users home page is located (e.g., wwwsb.ccsu.ctstateu.edu/faculty/frost/460).
Host	A host is a computer on the Web. The term is used interchangeably with site.
HTML	An abbreviation for HyperText Markup Language, the common language used to write documents that appear on the World Wide Web.
HTTP	An abbreviation for HyperText Transport Protocol, the common protocol used to communicate between World Wide Web servers.
Hyperlink	Hyperlinks are text or graphics that link to other pages on the Web.

Hypertext	This refers to text elements within a document that have an embedded connection to another item. Web documents use hypertext links to access documents, images, sounds, and video files from the Internet. The term hyperlink is a general term that applies to elements on Web pages other than text.
Internet	The Internet is the global inter-network of computers. Major uses of the Internet include e-mail and Web browsing.
Intranet	Intranets employ Internet technology to form home pages that are internal to a company. The Intranet serves as an easily accessible repository for corporate information—anything from strategic targets to health plans. Intranets capitalize on the fact that most organizations distribute far more information internally than they do to the outside world.
ISP	Internet Service Providers are companies that sell access to the Internet.
Java	This is an object-oriented programming language developed by Sun Microsystems.
JavaScript	This is a scripting language developed by Netscape in cooperation with Sun Microsystems to add functionality to the basic Web page. It is not as powerful as Java and works primarily from the client side.
LAN	A Local Area Network connects computers in an organization allowing them to communicate and share resources such as printers and Internet connections.
Link	See hyperlink
Modem	A modem is a device that translates computer signals into sound waves and back again to allow two computers to communicate over a phone line. Its name comes from the fact that it modulates computer signals to sound and demodulates sound back to computer signals. Today's fastest modems receive data at about 50,000 characters per second.
Mosaic	This is the name of the browser that was created at the National Center for Supercomputing Applications. It was the first Web browser to have a consistent interface for the Macintosh, Windows, and UNIX environments. The success of this browser is responsible for the expansion of the Web.
Net	Net is short for Internet.
Newsgroup	This the name for the discussion groups that can be on the Usenet. Not all news groups are accessible through the Internet. Some are accessible only through a modem connection. (See Usenet.)
Open text search	An open text search looks for word matches when given a search string.
Plug-in	This is a resource that is added to Netscape to extend its basic function.

QuickTime	This is a format used by Apple Computer to make, view, edit, and send digital audio and video.
Server	This is a software program used to provide, or serve, information to remote computers. Servers function in a Client-Server information exchange model. This term may also be loosely applied to the computer that is used to serve the information. (See Client.)
Site	A site is a computer on the Internet. Site is also used to refer to a home page (e.g., "great Web site").
Subject tree search	A subject tree search requires that the user navigate by progressively more specific subjects until they find the information for which they are looking.
T1	A T1 line is a high-speed telecommunications line used by larger organizations. T1 lines have 24 64 Kbps channels. A fractional T1 line uses only some of the available channels.
Table	This refers to a specific formatting element found in HTML pages. Tables are used on HTML documents to visually organize information.
Telnet	This is the process of remotely connecting and using a computer at a distant location.
Upload	This is the process of moving or transferring a document, file, or program from one computer to another computer.
URL	This is an abbreviation for Universal Resource Locator. In its basic sense it is an address used by people on the Internet to locate documents. URLs have a common format that describes the protocol for information transfer, the host computer address, the path to the desired file, and the name of the file requested.
Usenet	This is a world-wide system of discussion groups, also called newsgroups. There are many thousands of newsgroups, but only a percentage of these are accessible from the Internet.
WAN	Wide Area Networks (WANs) connect different divisions of an organization that are located across the city, across the country, or across the world from one another.
Web (WWW)	The World Wide Web (WWW) defines a standard for navigating between computers on the Internet using hyperlinks.